International

Book of

Tennis Drills

D0062646

International Book of Tennis Drills

Over 100 Skill-Specific Drills Adopted
by Tennis Professionals Worldwide

By the United States
Professional Tennis Registry

TRIUMPH BOOKS
Chicago

International Standard Book Number: 1-880141-36-1

For more information on the USPTR, contact:

United States Professional Tennis Registry
P.O. Box 4739
Hilton Head Island, South Carolina 29938
(800) 421-6289 or (803) 785-7244
Fax: (803) 686-2033

This book is available in quantity at special discounts for
your group or organization. For further information, contact:

Triumph Books
644 South Clark Street, Suite 2000
Chicago, Illinois 60605
(312) 939-3330
Fax: (312) 663-3557

Drills by Dennis Van der Meer and Ken DeHart
Cover design by Sam Concialdi
Typography and design by Jeff Dalpiaz

Printed in the United States of America

Library of Congress Cataloging-in-Publication Data
International book of tennis drills : over 100 skill-specific
drills adopted by tennis professionals worldwide / by the
United States Professional Tennis Registry.
     p.   cm.
  ISBN 1-880141-36-1 : $14.95
  1. Tennis — Coaching.   I. United States Professional
Tennis Registry
GV1002.9.C63I58   1993   93-7915
796.342'07'7 — dc20   CIP

Introduction

The United States Professional Tennis Registry's International Book of Drills has been created with both the tennis coach and the tennis-teaching professional in mind. The description of each drill is divided into four distinct categories:

1) Skill objectives of each drill
2) Procedural requirements
3) Sequence of shot progressions
4) Ideas for variety with each drill

A graphic illustration of each drill appears on the page adjoining the description.

The International Book of Drills is by no means a complete compendium of every tennis drill known. It should, however, serve as a catalyst for the tennis coach's imagination, thereby prompting numerous variations of the drills at hand.

The drills are grouped in a manner which allows for easy reference and consultation. Because the drills are separated into 12 sections, it makes it easy for the tennis teacher or coach to use certain drills for specific on-court situations.

As you read through the drills, please note that the vertical black bar on each left-hand page indicates what general section of the book you are reading. The right-hand pages contain the specific drill itself, with the illustration and drill name on each page.

The sections are intended to make teaching tennis easier by dividing the game of tennis into smaller components easily understood by the teacher and the student.

The drills in the beginning of the book provide excellent instruction for the proper mechanics of each stroke — the serve, forehand, backhand, volley, lob and overhead. These pages should be studied first to provide a solid foundation of the fundamental tennis strokes using bio-mechanically correct movement.

The sections in the back of this book provide detailed drills for more-advanced players. The sections regarding the singles and doubles match-play tactics should be used only after the student has had enough experience and practice learning the basics of the strokes.

Also, the Speed and Agility section provides effective drills to enhance on-court movement of any tennis player.

The ball machine drills can be made more challenging or less challenging, depending on the skill level of the student. By altering the depth, speed and direction of the feeds, the ball machine drills can be adjusted to fit the needs of each individual player. These drills can also be changed by increasing or decreasing the interval of time which elapses between feeds.

Several pages are reserved at the end of the book for your personal notes and drill diagrams.

We sincerely hope that the International Book of Drills can help to further both your enjoyment of tennis as well as your enthusiasm for tennis teaching.

As president and founder of the USPTR, I would like to acknowledge the help of the many members worldwide whose contributions have made the International Book of Drills a reality.

Best wishes to all,

Dennis Van der Meer

Dennis Van der Meer

The USPTR

The USPTR was established in 1976 to certify tennis teachers through an internationally-recognized test based on a standardized teaching method. Development of this method began when Dennis Van der Meer and Billie Jean King began a tennis camp in 1972, and saw a need for an introductory method to teaching.

While most tennis experts agree that though there are many different ways to teach tennis, the concept of a worldwide teaching standard is sound. In today's transient, extremely mobile society, tennis players should be able to continue to develop their basic skills without being subject to the whims of each individual pro.

Today, the USPTR boasts more than 7,000 tennis teachers in more than 100 countries who are certified to teach tennis using a biomechanically-sound method.

In order to become certified by the USPTR, a written and on-court examination must be taken. The written portion covers knowledge of tactics and strategy, as well as teaching and corrective techniques. The on-court tests examine the ability of the instructor to demonstrate strokes and to conduct a class in a real teaching situation. In the skills test, ball control, placement, and specialty shot execution must be demonstrated. In the teaching test, the instructor must teach a group and a private lesson.

The highest rating, that of Professional, is achieved when the applicant scores a Professional rating on each of the three portions of the certification test: written, skills and teaching. A lesser rating on any portion of the test may qualify the applicant for an Instructor or Associate Instructor rating.

Applicants may attempt to upgrade their rating after a 30-day waiting period. USPTR Tennis Teacher Workshops are held worldwide in many languages. Certification sites and Testers are also located around the world.

Table of Contents

A short warm-up period is recommended before starting any of the drills in this book.

Caution and safety are always a top priority whenever players are gathered on a tennis court.

List of Drills

List of Drills

Service
Game

SKILL OBJECTIVE

- Bio-mechanically sound service motion with emphasis on form rather than power.

PROCEDURE

- 2-4 servers stand facing the net on one end of the court about 6' away from the net.
- One player waits behind each server to rotate in after every two serves.
- Ball basket is located at the center of the service line on the servers' end of the court.

SEQUENCE

- Servers stand sideways to the net and put their rackets on their shoulders in preparation to serve.
- Servers then toss the ball into the air, swing and hit.
- After 2 serves each, servers switch with players waiting to rotate in.
- As players develop sound mechanics for executing the toss, swing and hit; repeat the same sequence from the service line, then from 3/4 court, then from the baseline.

FOR VARIETY

- Players may practice their serves before the drill begins.
- Repeat the same sequence using a full service motion (down together, up together) starting from the service line and progressing to the baseline.

The Serve

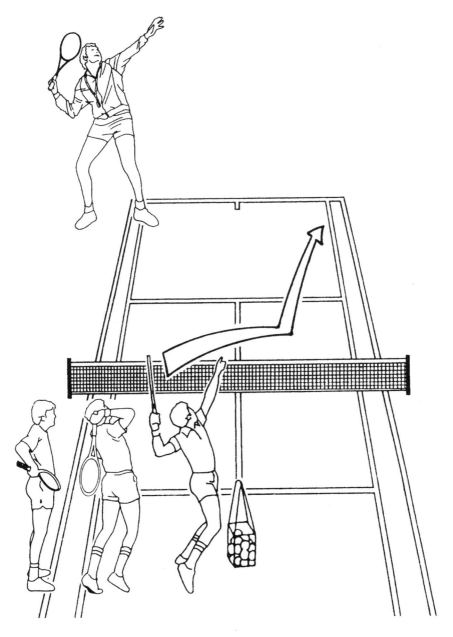

SKILL OBJECTIVES

- Serving to the opponent's backhand.
- Automatic response in match play.
- Accuracy under pressure.

PROCEDURE

- A towel is placed as a target in the backhand corner of both service blocks on one end of the court.
- Two servers serve from the opposite end of the court.
- A basket of balls is placed behind the baseline within easy reach between the two servers.

SEQUENCE

- The two servers serve at the same time, aiming for the backhand target on each serve.
- The servers are serving to score points against the target, not against each other.
- For each serve, the server scores one point for hitting the towel. The towel scores a point if the server misses.
- Servers rotate after every two serves to gain experience serving to the backhand from the deuce and ad courts.
- Players slowly learn to score points against the target and eventually win games.

FOR VARIETY

- Add two receivers to return the serves. This will put more pressure on the servers to maintain their concentration.

Server vs. Target

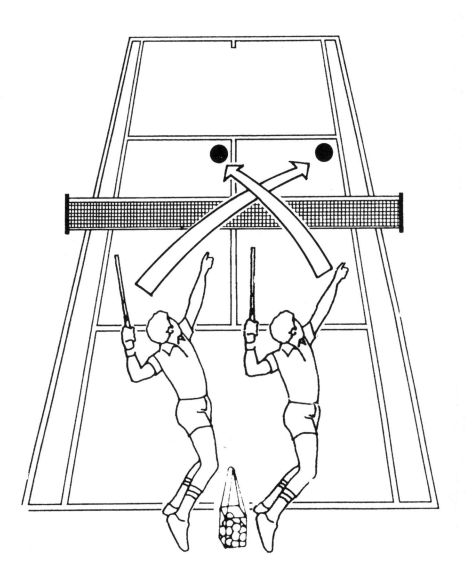

SKILL OBJECTIVES

- Direction and placement of serves.
- Depth of serves.
- Velocity of serves.

PROCEDURE

- Service blocks are divided vertically and horizontally into four quadrants with ball can lids or other visible markers.
- Two servers serve at a time from the opposite baseline, alternating from the ad side to the deuce side after every two serves.

SEQUENCE

- One server declares in advance whether the serve will be directed to the forehand or backhand.
- Players serve two balls from each side, scoring one point for each accurately-placed serve.
- The other server declares the direction of the next serve, etc., as players continue to switch sides after every two serves until one player wins by scoring a total of 20 points.
- Repeat the same sequence, only this time serving for depth. Serves must land in the deep corner of the service block, directed to the forehand or backhand quadrant as decided in advance. The first player to score 20 points wins.
- The next step is to add pace. Following the same sequence as before, servers score three points for each accurately-placed serve which hits the fence before the second bounce, two points if the second bounce is beyond the baseline, one point if the second bounce is within the playing court, and no points if the serve is not accurately placed. Advanced players may be required to subtract one point for each serve that misses the service block altogether.

Serving for Depth

SKILL OBJECTIVES

- Closing in behind the serve.
- Consistency and placement of passing down the line.
- Moving to cover the open court.

PROCEDURE

- Server is in position to serve from the deuce court.
- Receiver is in position to return serve from the opposite deuce court.

SEQUENCE

- Server serves, closes in and splits.
- Receiver hits return of serve down the line and gets set to respond to the direction of the ball.
- Server volleys crosscourt.
- Receiver moves left to cover the open court and hits backhand passing shot down the line for a winner.

FOR VARIETY

- Reverse: Repeat the same sequence from the ad court to develop consistency on both forehand and backhand sides.
- Place targets near the baseline in both the deuce and ad corners of the court. Players aim for the target when hitting passing shots down the line.

SERVICE GAME

14

Serve and Follow
the Ball

Service Return

SKILL OBJECTIVE

- Consistency and placement of service returns down the line.

PROCEDURE

- Two servers stand inside the service line about 6' from the net, one on the ad side and one on the deuce side of the court.
- Two receivers stand on the opposite service line, one on the ad side and one on the deuce side.
- Two players wait in line behind the receivers to rotate in.
- Ball basket is located at the center of the service line between the two feeders.

SEQUENCE

- Both servers serve to their respective receivers at the same time by tapping a ball so that it lands halfway between the service line and net, in front of the receiver.
- Each receiver returns the ball down the line away from the server.
- After one return each, receivers switch with players waiting to rotate in.
- After 10 serves each, servers rotate to become receivers and two receivers replace the servers.
- The same sequence is then repeated.

FOR VARIETY

- As players develop consistency in returning serves down the line, both servers and receivers move back to 3/4 court, then to the baseline.
- Receivers alternate returning serves from both the deuce and ad side of the court. Servers serve from both sides.

Return of Serve

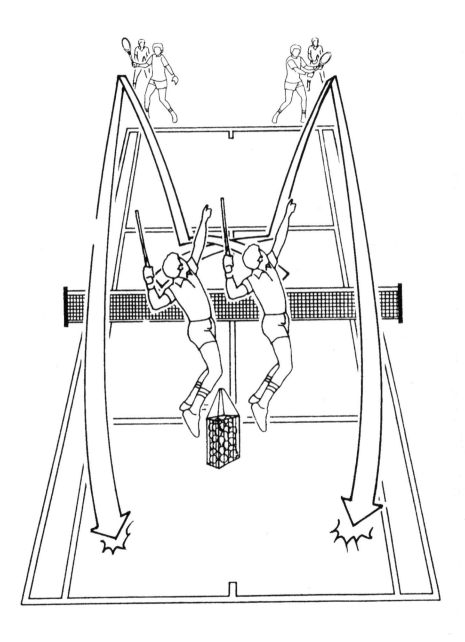

SKILL OBJECTIVES

- Quick reaction time on fast, hard serves.
- Wrist snap on the serve.
- Quick footwork and short backswing on the return of serve.

PROCEDURE

- Two servers are positioned on the service line.
- Two receivers are in position to return serve from the other end of the court — one from the deuce court, one from the ad court.

SEQUENCE

- Both servers serve crosscourt at the same time.
- Receivers return serves down the line.
- After 10 serves, players rotate so that servers become receivers and receivers become servers. Each player should have a turn serving and receiving from both the deuce and the ad side of the court.

FOR VARIETY

- To improve eye contact and footwork, have receivers catch the serves with two hands instead of returning serve with the racket.
- Have receivers return serve down the alley line instead of crosscourt.
- As the players' skill level improves, have servers serve from halfway between the service line and the baseline.

20

Quick Return of Serve

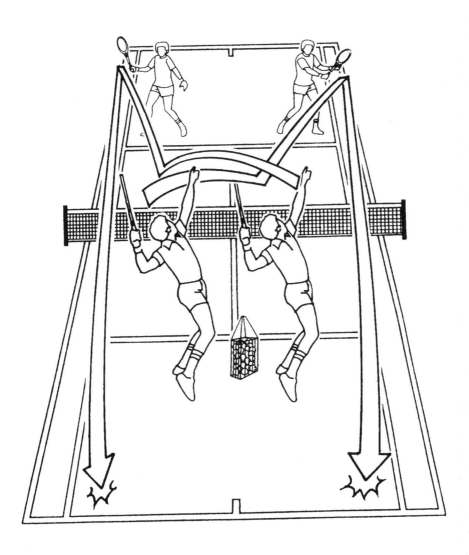

SKILL OBJECTIVES

- Consistency and placement of service returns.
- Steadiness and precision in groundstroke rallies.
- Putting the first serve into play.

PROCEDURE

- Two players are in position to serve from one end of the court, one on the deuce side and one on the ad side.
- Two players are in position to return serve from the opposite end of the court.
- Two players wait behind the receivers to rotate into position to return serve.
- Ball basket is located between the servers.

SEQUENCE

- Both servers serve simultaneously to their respective receivers.
- Receivers return the serves down the line and players rally groundstrokes down the line for a maximum of 10 hits. GROUNDSTROKES ONLY. NO LOBS ALLOWED. ALL SHOTS MUST LAND BEHIND TIIE SERVICE LINE. BALL MUST BE HIT AFTER ONE BOUNCE ONLY.
- Receivers alternate with players waiting to rotate in after each point.
- After 10 serves and returns, players rotate so that servers become receivers and vice versa.

FOR VARIETY

- Doubles alley may be used in rallying.
- Players hit only forehands or only backhands.
- Servers alternate serving from the deuce and ad side of the court.

Serve, Return and Rally

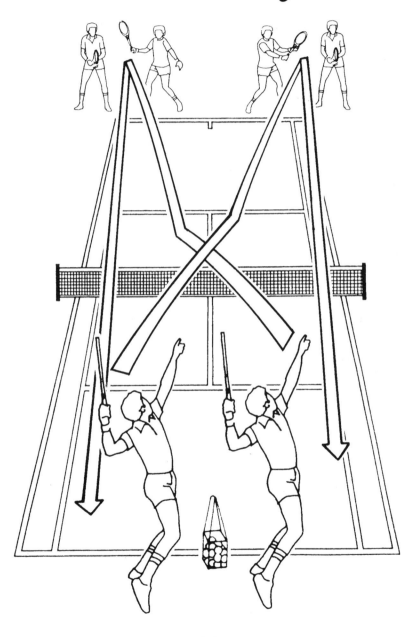

Groundstrokes

SKILL OBJECTIVES

- Bio-mechanically sound technique on forehand and backhand groundstrokes.
- Consistency and placement of groundstrokes down the line.

PROCEDURE

- Two groundstrokers stand on the service line at one end of the court, one on the ad side and one on the deuce side.
- Two feeders stand about 6' away from the net, opposite the groundstrokers.
- Ball baskets are located between the feeders.

SEQUENCE

- Both feeders feed to their respective groundstrokers at the same time so that the balls land inside the service line in front of the groundstrokers.
- Groundstrokers return the ball down the line. (Ad court player hits backhands; deuce court player hits forehands.)
- After 10 hits, players rotate so that feeders become groundstrokers and groundstrokers become feeders.
- As players develop sound mechanics and stroke consistency, players repeat the same sequence from 3/4 court, and then, from the baseline.
- After completing the sequence from the baseline, ad and deuce court players switch sides and the same sequence is repeated again, starting back at the service line.

Groundstroke Drill

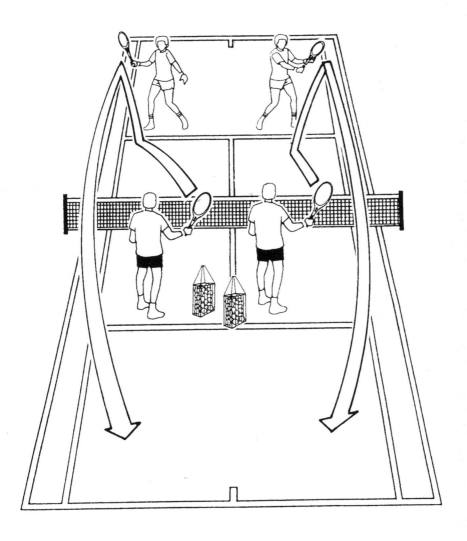

SKILL OBJECTIVES

- Hitting groundstrokes on the run.
- Hitting under pressure.

PROCEDURE

- Players are divided into two groups, one group on each end of the court.
- Players in each group are lined up behind the center of the baseline.
- Ball basket is located near the back fence on one end of the court designated as the feed end.

SEQUENCE

- First player in line on the feed end starts the ball into play by feeding to the opponent, then runs to the end of the opposite line, running around the length of the court in a counter-clockwise direction.
- Opponent returns the ball with a groundstroke, then runs to the end of the opposite line.
- Next players in line attempt to keep the rally going, with each hitter in line rotating to the opposite end of the court after one hit each.
- When a player misses, a new ball is put into play by the hitter on the feed end and the rally continues.
- When a player commits two errors, he or she must drop out.
- The rally continues until only two players remain.
- The last two players do not rotate ends but play out the point to determine the winner.

FOR VARIETY

- Ball must land behind the service line to count.
- Players hit only forehands or only backhands.

Around the World

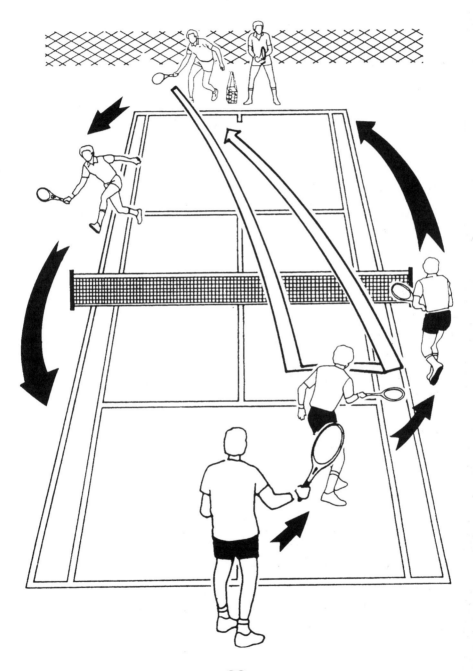

SKILL OBJECTIVES

- Consistency and placement of groundstrokes.
- Hitting for depth.

PROCEDURE (6 players)

- Players are divided into two teams, one team on each end of the court.
- Two players from each team play at a time from the baseline, one on the deuce side and one on the ad side.
- The third player on each team waits at the back fence until time to enter.
- Pro feeds from outside the ad court alley, near the service line.

SEQUENCE

- Pro starts the ball into play by feeding across the net deep into the deuce court.
- Deuce court player returns the ball to either opponent and players play out the point using only groundstrokes and hitting for depth. ALL SHOTS MUST LAND BETWEEN THE BASELINE AND SERVICE LINE, OTHERWISE THE BALL IS "OUT!"
- When one player misses, the player who has missed goes back to the fence and is replaced by the "third" player who has been waiting to enter.
- Teams compete for specified points, then switch ends.

FOR VARIETY

- To emphasize control and placement: Before either team may attempt to win the point, players must sustain a controlled rally until all four players have hit the ball at least once. Players on each team rotate clockwise after every two points.

Brazilian
Baseline Drill

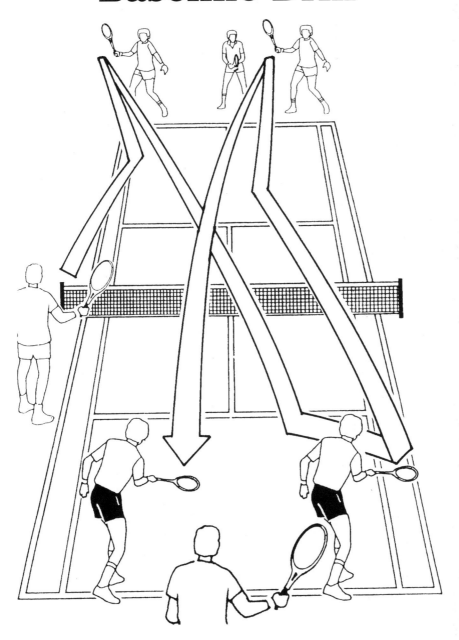

SKILL OBJECTIVES

- Controlling the direction and placement of the ball.
- Hitting an angle off a down-the-line shot.

PROCEDURE

- Pro is at the net in the ad court.
- Pro's partner is on the baseline in the pro's deuce court.
- Two players are on the opposite baseline, one in the deuce court, one in the ad court.

SEQUENCE

- Pro feeds ball across the net to ad court.
- Ad court player hits groundstroke down the line to pro's partner.
- Pro's partner returns the ball down the line.
- Ad court player hits crosscourt to pro.
- Pro volleys to deuce court player.
- Deuce court player hits crosscourt.
- Pro introduces new feed and the sequence is repeated.

FOR VARIETY

- Rather than introducing a new feed each time, have players keep one ball in play as long as possible, repeating the same sequence of shots until someone misses.
- Reverse: Pro feeds from deuce court. Pro's partner is at the baseline in the ad court. Pro will feed to deuce court player and the shot sequence will remain the same but in reverse.

GROUNDSTROKES

Change of Angle

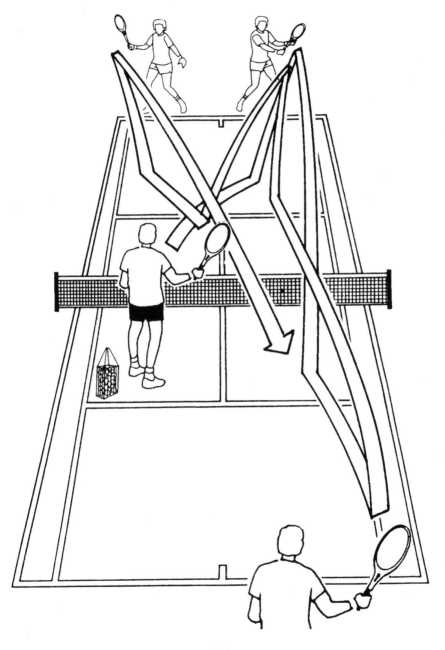

SKILL OBJECTIVES

- Consistency and directional control.
- Ability to maintain concentration.
- Ability to enter concentration quickly.

PROCEDURE (6 players)

- Two hitters are on each baseline, one in the deuce court, one in the ad court
- Odd player on each end waits back at the fence with extra balls.

SEQUENCE

- Hitters on one end start the ball into play crosscourt with a drop-and-hit.
- Hitters rally crosscourt until one player misses.
- Odd player on that end steps in and takes the place of the hitter who has missed, starting new ball into play by feeding to the opponent crosscourt.
- Hitter who has been replaced goes back to the fence, gets ball, and waits for turn to re-enter.

FOR VARIETY

- Players play out the rally point down the line rather than crosscourt.
- Teams keep score and compete to win.

Odd Player In

SKILL OBJECTIVES

- Changing direction and keeping the ball under control.
- Passing shot down the line.

PROCEDURE

- Pro feeds from the deuce court service line.
- Players are lined up across the net from the pro behind the ad court alley.
- Target is located 3' inside the baseline at the singles sideline of the pro's ad court.

SEQUENCE

- Pro feeds ball to player's forehand.
- Player hits forehand down the line to pro and continues to move toward the center of the baseline.
- Pro feeds ball to player's backhand.
- Player moves back toward the ad court alley and hits backhand down the line to pro.
- Pro feeds third ball deep to hitter's deuce court.
- Player runs to ball and hits forehand passing shot down the line, aiming for target.

FOR VARIETY

- Reverse: Players line up behind deuce court, pro feeds from ad court, and player will finish with backhand down the line.
- Pro feeds from the middle of the court and player finishes with crosscourt passing shot instead of down the line.

Change of Direction

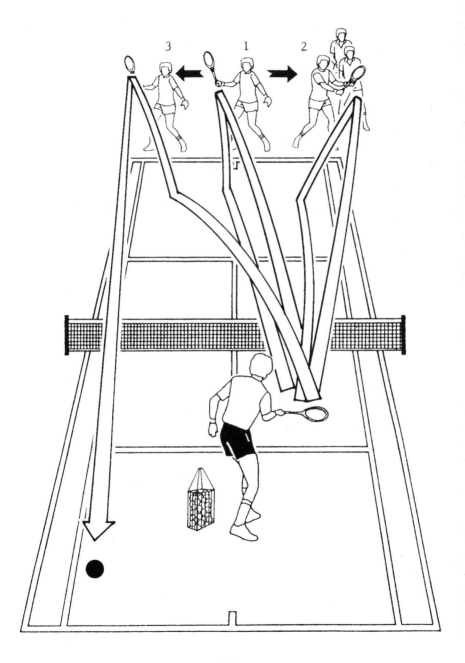

SKILL OBJECTIVES

- Proper positioning for control of groundstrokes.
- Controlled direction and placement.

PROCEDURE

- Players rally in pairs, one player at each end of the doubles alley.

SEQUENCE

- Players rally within the alley, attempting to keep one ball in play.
- For each shot landing within the alley, the hitter scores one point.
- The first player to score 11 points wins.
- Either player may introduce a new feed if the ball goes out so that the rally can continue without interrupting the rhythm of the rally.

FOR VARIETY

- Players rally forehand to forehand.
- Players rally backhand to backhand.
- Players alternate forehands and backhands.
- Players' choice of forehand or backhand on each shot.
- Rotate players to change partners after any one player scores 11 points.
- Players rally with the same partner until the pair achieves 10 to 20 successes without a miss. The scoring starts at zero each time either player misses the alley and a new ball is introduced.

GROUNDSTROKES

Alley Rally

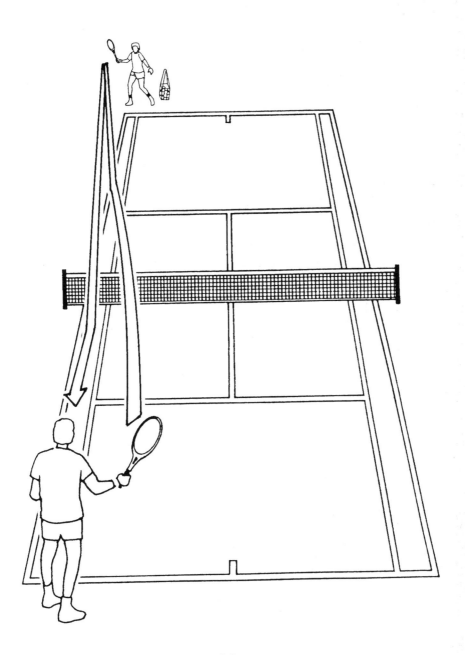

SKILL OBJECTIVES

- Hitting on the move.
- Accuracy of passing shots.
- Hit-and-recovery footwork.

PROCEDURE

- Players line up in two lines at the center of the baseline.
- Players in line behind the hitters shadow the motions of the hitter.
- Targets are placed in the deuce and ad corners of the pro's court.
- Pro feeds from the center service line across the net from the players.

SEQUENCE

- Pro feeds to deuce court.
- Hitter A moves to the right and hits down the line, aiming for target.
- Hitter and shadows side-hop to starting position.
- Pro feeds to ad court.
- Hitter B moves left and hits down the line to deuce court target.
- Hitter and shadows side-hop back to starting position.
- Hitter A goes to the end of line B. Hitter B goes to the end of line A. Drill continues in the same sequence as players rotate from one line to the other.

FOR VARIETY

- Players strive to achieve 3'-5' net clearance on each shot to increase percentage of success.
- Players aim for crosscourt target rather than hitting down the line.
- Hitters go to pick up balls before rotating to end of the line.

Passing Shots

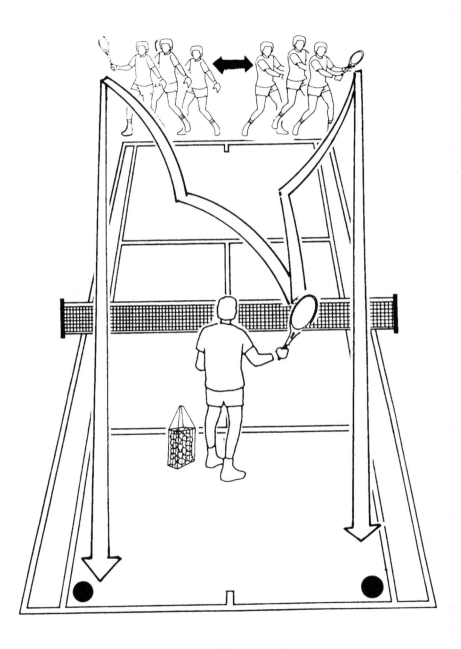

SKILL OBJECTIVES

- Consistency and placement of groundstrokes.
- Movement side-to-side, corner to corner.

PROCEDURE

- One player is on each end of the court in starting position at the center of the baseline.

SEQUENCE

- One player starts the ball into play with a drop-and-hit deep dcwn the line to the opponent.
- Opponent moves wide into position to return the ball and hits crosscourt.
- First player runs wide and hits the ball back down the line.
- Players continue to rally, groundstroke-to-groundstroke, with the first player hitting all the shots down the line and the second player hitting all shots crosscourt. (Both players will be alternating forehands and backhands.)
- When one player misses, either player feeds a new ball into play to continue the rally with as little interruption as possible.
- After a period of time, players switch so that the player who was hitting down the line hits crosscourt and vice versa.

FOR VARIETY

- Players attempt to keep one ball in play for a specified number of hits (10-20 each).
- Players increase depth and pace to try to force the opponent to make an error. Compete to win 11 or 21 points with a two-point margin.

Baseline to Baseline

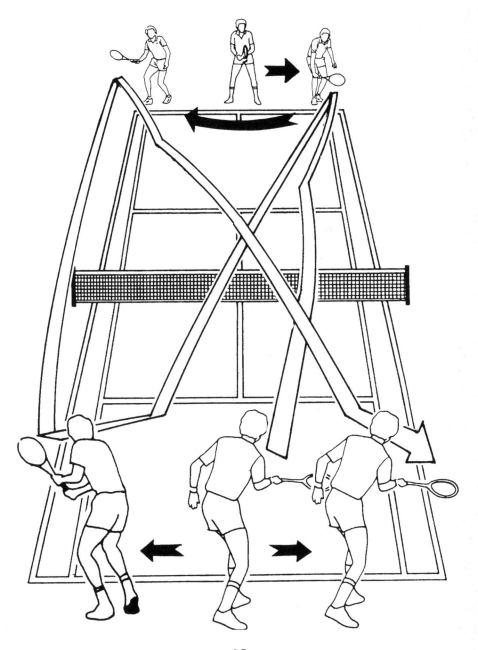

SKILL OBJECTIVES

- Lateral movement
- Short-angle passing shots.
- Control and placement of groundstrokes.

PROCEDURE

- Players are lined up behind the center of the baseline.
- Pro feeds from across the net at the center of the service line.
- Targets are placed in the deep wide corners of the deuce and ad court service blocks on the pro's end of the court.

SEQUENCE

- Pro feeds wide ball deep into the deuce court.
- First player in line runs wide to the right and hits short-angle forehand passing shot crosscourt, aiming for deuce court target.
- Pro feeds wide ball deep into the ad court.
- Player runs wide to the left and hits short-angle backhand passing shot crosscourt, aiming for ad court target.
- Player rotates to the end of the line and the next player in line repeats the same sequence.

SEQUENCE

- Player hits forehand deep down the line and target.
- Player hits short-angle forehand crosscourt to target and backhand deep down the line.
- Reverse: Repeat the same sequences in reverse, feeding first to the ad court, then to the deuce court.

Singapore Swing

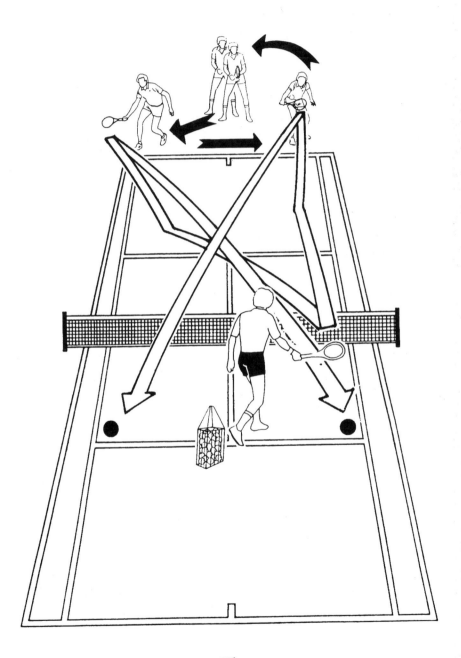

SKILL OBJECTIVES

- Returns used in doubles play.
- Quick footwork to move to the ball.
- Inside-out passing shots.

PROCEDURE

- Players are lined up in two lines, starting at the intersection of the baseline and singles sidelines.
- The first player in each line is the hitter. Other players shadow the motions of the hitter.
- Pro feeds from across the net, 2' inside the service line on the center line.
- Targets are placed in the deep corners of the deuce and ad court service blocks, next to the sidelines to the right and left of the pro.

SEQUENCE

- Pro feeds deep ball just into the deuce side of the court.
- Hitter A moves to the ball using small quick steps and returns the ball crosscourt, aiming for the deuce court target.
- Pro feeds deep ball up the middle into ad court.
- Hitter B moves to the ball and hits crosscourt return to ad court target.
- Repeat the sequence as next players rotate to the head of each line and hitters rotate from one line to the other, going to the end of the line to shadow the motions of the next hitter.

FOR VARIETY

- Move targets back to the baseline and have players hit crosscourt returns deep into the corners.
- Move targets back to baseline and have players hit returns down the line for depth, aiming for targets.

Doubles Passing Shots

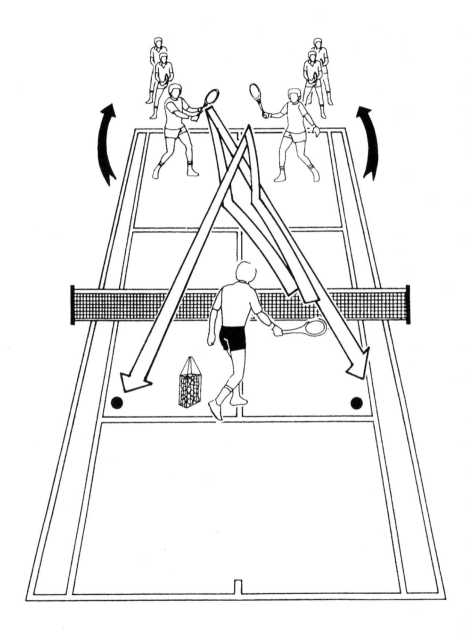

SKILL OBJECTIVES

- Movement to retrieve high deep balls.
- Movement to and through short balls.
- Movement up and back in the court.

PROCEDURE

- Players line up in starting position at the center of the baseline.
- Pro feeds from across the net near the center of the court.

SEQUENCE

- Pro feeds high ball deep into player's deuce court.
- Player backs up and returns high ball over the net.
- Pro feeds short low ball to deuce court.
- Player moves up and hits short ball crosscourt.
- Pro feeds deep and high to player's ad court.
- Player runs back to retrieve high ball and returns it across the net.
- Pro feeds short ball to ad court.
- Player moves in and hits short ball crosscourt.
- Repeat for 20 balls.

FOR VARIETY

- Players practice topspin lobs on deep balls. Hit short balls down the line.
- Hit all four balls as passing shots — very aggressively.

Yo Yo

SKILL OBJECTIVES

- Reflex, ability to think and act quickly.
- Control and placement of groundstrokes.

PROCEDURE

- 2-4 players line up one behind the other behind each baseline.
- Only the first player in each line has a racket.

SEQUENCE

- The first player in line on one end of the court drops and hits the ball across the net to the opponent, then passes the racket to the next player in line and rotates to the end of the line.
- First hitter on the other end of the court returns the ball with a groundstroke then passes the racket to the next player in line and rotates to the end of the line.
- Players continue the rally, trying to keep one ball in play for as long as possible, each player passing the racket to the next after one hit and rotating to the end of the line.
- When one player misses, a new feed is introduced immediately by the hitter on the opposing team.

FOR VARIETY

- Teams compete to win a designated number of points.
- All hits must land behind the service line for depth or the team loses the point.
- Repeat the same drill from the service line.

Pass the Racket

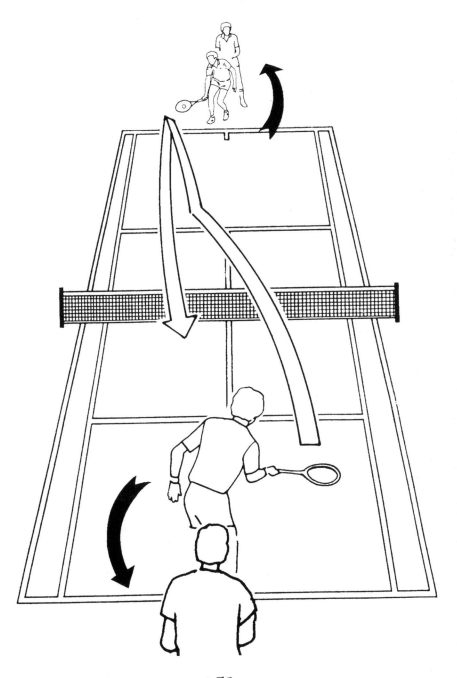

Midcourt Shots

SKILL OBJECTIVES

- Crosscourt placement of midcourt shots.
- Movement.
- Acceleration upward to hit short ball hard.
- Opening up the court.

PROCEDURE

- Players line up in two lines behind the center of the service line.
- The player at the head of each line is the hitter. Other players shadow the motions of the hitters.
- Pro feeds from the center of the service line opposite the players.
- Targets are located halfway between the net and service line, next to the singles sideline in the pro's deuce and ad court.

SEQUENCE

- Pro feeds into deuce court service block.
- Hitter in line A moves to the ball using small quick steps and hits with exaggerated topspin crosscourt, aiming for deuce court target.
- Hitter then recovers to the center of the court.
- Pro feeds into ad court service block.
- Hitter in line B moves to the ball using quick small steps, hits with exaggerated topspin to ad court target, and recovers to starting position.
- Hitters rotate to the end of the opposite line after 10 shots.
- Repeat the same sequence, feeding alternately to the next two hitters for 10 shots each.

FOR VARIETY

- Two players go to pick up balls during each rotation.

Short Angle Kill Shot

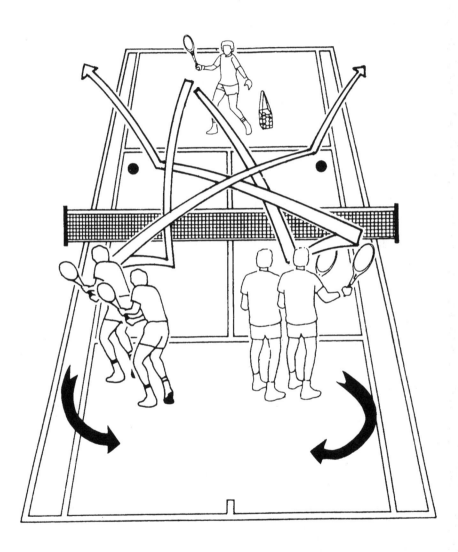

SKILL OBJECTIVES

- Down-the-line placement of midcourt shots.
- Moving to the ball.
- Acceleration forward to hit short ball hard.
- Putting the short ball away.

PROCEDURE

- Players line up in two lines behind center of the service line.
- The player at the head of each line is the hitter. Other players shadow the hitter's motion.
- Pro feeds from the center of the service line opposite the players.
- Targets are located deep in the deuce and ad corners of the pro's court, just inside the baseline.

SEQUENCE

- Pro feeds short ball into deuce court service block. Ball should land 3' inside service line.
- Hitter from line A moves to the baseline using small steps, and hits with exaggerated topspin down the line aiming for target, going for depth.
- Pro feeds into ad court service block.
- Hitter from line B follows the same sequence, hitting down the line to the deuce court target.
- Hitters recover to starting position after each shot and repeat the same sequence for 10 shots each.
- After a total of 10 shots each, hitters rotate to the end of the opposite line.
- Pro feeds alternately to next two hitters and the same sequence is repeated.

FOR VARIETY

- Two players go to pick up balls during each rotation.

Midcourt Kill Shot

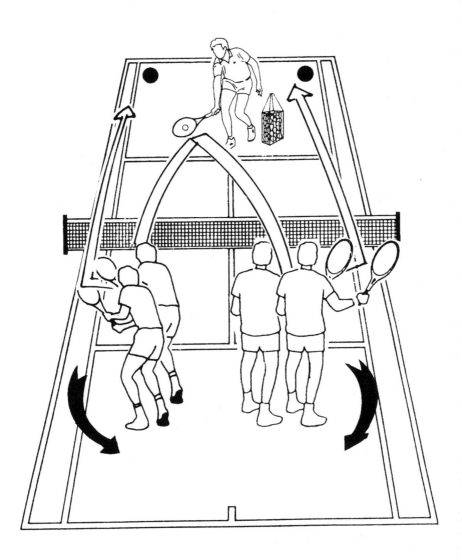

SKILL OBJECTIVES

- Hitting on the move.
- Reacting to the direction of the ball.
- Putting away the short ball.

PROCEDURE

- The hitter starts at the center of the court behind the baseline.
- Players lined up behind the hitter shadow the motions of the hitter.
- Pro feeds from across the net halfway between the service line and net on the center line.
- Two players are behind the pro's baseline to retrieve balls during each rotation.
- Targets are placed in the far corners of the pro's court on both the deuce and ad sides.

SEQUENCE

- Pro feeds four balls in sequence to the hitter, mixing up feeds to the forehand and backhand. The first three balls are fed deep and wide, the fourth ball is fed short so that the player must move in to close out the point.
- Hitter reacts to the direction of each feed and hits crosscourt or down the line, aiming for one target or the other on each shot.
- Hitter closes in on the short ball and puts it away to end the point.
- Players rotate.
- As players rotate, pro mixes up the pattern of feeds to the forehand and backhand so that each hitter must react to the direction of the feed, really stretch out, and hit on the move.

Guess Which Way

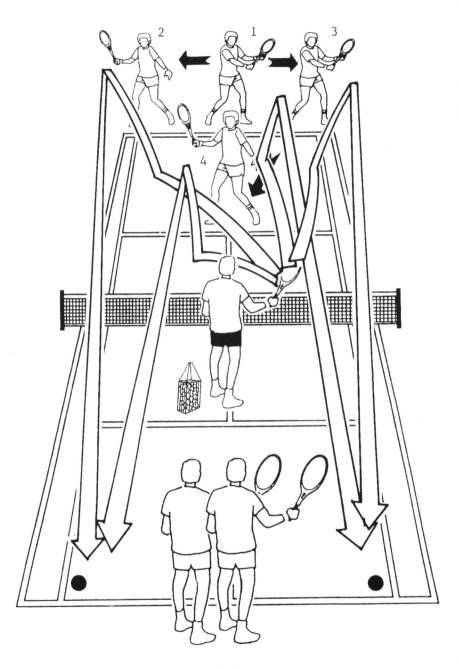

SKILL OBJECTIVES

- Consistent placement crosscourt and down the line.
- Moving the opponent side to side.
- Opening up the court and closing out the point.

PROCEDURE

- Server is in starting position at the baseline.
- Receiver is in the deuce court near the baseline across the net from the server.
- Pro feeds from the center of the baseline on the receiver's side of the court.

SEQUENCE

- Pro puts ball into play by feeding to server.
- Server hits wide crosscourt angle into receiver's deuce court.
- Receiver hits defensive shot down the line.
- Server attacks the receiver's return, hitting a wide crosscourt angle into the ad court and closing into the net.
- Receiver scrambles wide to the ad court and saves the point by hitting down the line.
- Server hits crosscourt angle volley into the open court to close out the point.

FOR VARIETY

- Receiver may try to save the point on the last shot. In this case, the server will have the option of trying to "wrong-foot" the receiver by hitting back down the line instead of crosscourt. The receiver must return all shots down the line. Play continues until one player falters by hitting short or high and loses the point.

Side-to-Side

Volleys

SKILL OBJECTIVES

- Quick reaction time in volley exchanges.
- Changing the direction of the ball with control.
- Keeping the ball in play.

PROCEDURE

- **Team 1:** 3 players are in volley position about 8' from the net on each end of the court, facing each other across the net in pairs — one pair near each singles sideline and one pair at the center line.
- **Team 2:** 3 players are at each end of the court at the service line, one behind each volleyer.

SEQUENCE

- Using only one ball and hitting volley-to-volley across the net, volleyers attempt to pass the ball from one sideline to the other and back again without a miss. One deuce court player hits the first volley to the ad court player directly across the net and each player in turn volleys to the next player across the net in sequence, as follows:

Forehand volley (feed) to ad player's backhand,
Backhand volley to center player's forehand,
Forehand volley to center player's backhand,
Backhand volley to ad player's forehand,
Forehand volley to ad player's backhand,
Backhand volley to center player's backhand,
Backhand volley to center player's forehand,
Forehand volley to feeder's backhand
Backhand volley to end the sequence.

- Team 1 is allowed TWO attempts to complete the sequence without a miss. Vollyers then rotate to the service line and Team 2 then competes for two attempts.

VOLLEYS

Pass It On

SKILL OBJECTIVES

- Hitting volleys while on the move.
- Keeping the ball in play.
- Footwork and concentration.

PROCEDURE

- Two volleyers are in starting position across the net from each other near the singles sideline, about 8' from the net.
- Other players wait behind the volleyers at the service line until time to rotate into starting position.

SEQUENCE

- One volleyer starts the ball into play by feeding the ball across the net to the other.
- The other volleyer volleys the ball back and the two volleyers attempt to keep the ball in play, hitting volley-to-volley, as they move laterally across the court from one singles sideline to the other.
- As the first two volleyers reach the center service line, the next two volleyers in line move into starting position and begin the same sequence.
- As players reach the far sideline, they rotate to the opposite service line and wait in line to repeat the drill again, as players continue to rotate and the drill continues.

FOR VARIETY

- Players on one side of the net hit forehand volleys only and players on the other side hit backhand volleys only.
- Players volley forehand-to-forehand.
- Players volley backhand-to-backhand.

VOLLEYS

66

Lateral Movement Volleys

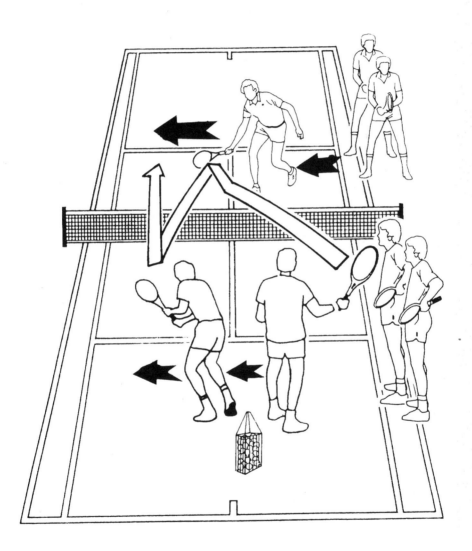

SKILL OBJECTIVES

- Overhead smash.
- Closing in to the net.
- Low volleys.

PROCEDURE

- Net player is halfway between the service line and net.
- Pro feeds from the baseline directly opposite the player.

SEQUENCE

- Pro feeds lob to net player.
- Net player hits overhead smash down the line to the pro.
- Pro hits low return.
- Net player closes in and hits low volley back to pro.
- Pro lobs and the sequence is repeated.

FOR VARIETY

- Play out the point after the net player has made the low volley.
- Repeat the High-Low sequence until the net player has hit 20 shots.

High-Low

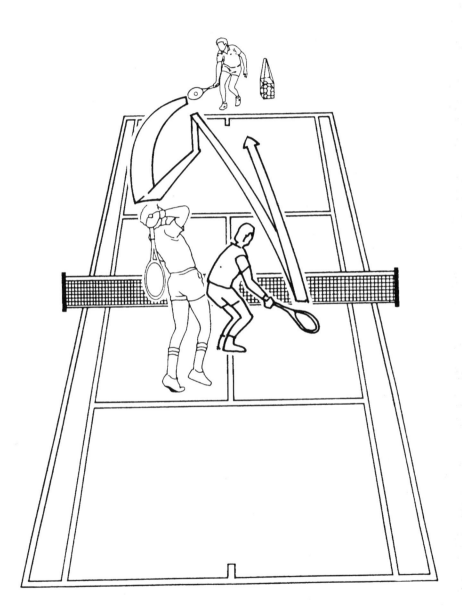

SKILL OBJECTIVES

- Footwork and movement at the net.
- Placement of short angle volleys.

PROCEDURE

- Players are lined up behind the center of the service line.
- Pro feeds from the center of the opposite service line.
- Targets are placed in the deep wide corners of the ad and deuce court service blocks, to the left and right of the pro.

SEQUENCE

- Pro feeds first ball to the deuce court.
- First player in line crosses in, steps, and hits short angle forehand volley crosscourt to target.
- Pro feeds second ball to ad court.
- Player reacts to the direction of the ball, moves over to cut off the ball and hits short angle backhand volley crosscourt, aiming for ad court target.
- Player rotates to the end of the line and the next player in line repeats the same two-volley sequence.

FOR VARIETY

- Player hits the forehand volley deep down the line and hits backhand volley.
- Player angles forehand volley crosscourt and hits backhand volley deep down the line.
- Reverse: Repeat the same drill in reverse. Pro feeds first to ad court, then to deuce court.

Criss-Cross Volleys

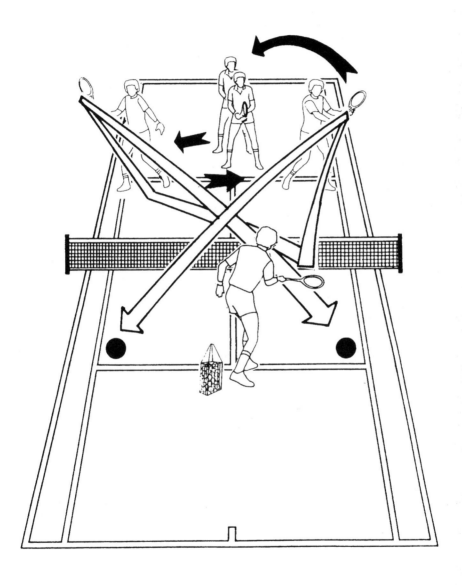

SKILL OBJECTIVES

- Low volleys.
- High volleys.
- Placement of volleys down the line.

PROCEDURE

- Players are lined up behind the center of the baseline.
- Pro feeds from the center of the opposite baseline.
- Target is located in the deep corner of the pro's ad court.

SEQUENCE

- First player in line runs in to the service line and takes split step as pro begins to feed the first ball.
- Pro feeds low volley to player's forehand.
- Player hits low volley down the line and continues closing in.
- Pro feeds high volley to player's forehand.
- Player hits high volley down the line, aiming for target.
- Player rotates to the end of the line and the next player in line repeats the same sequence.

FOR VARIETY

- Reverse: The same sequence is repeated in reverse. Players hit backhand volleys instead of forehand volleys and aim for target placed in the deep corner of the deuce court.

Low-High

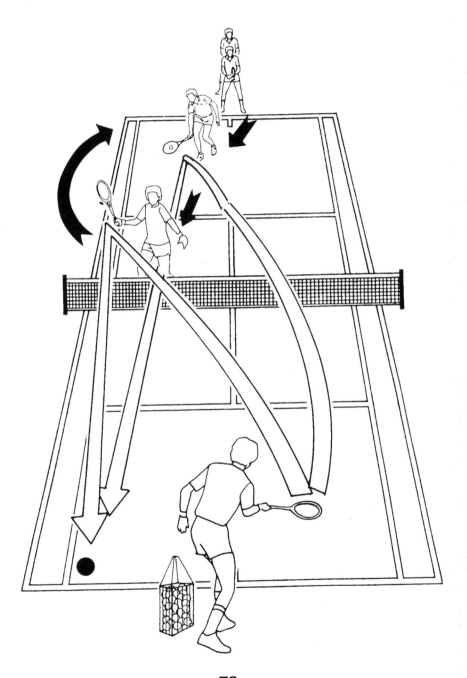

SKILL OBJECTIVES

- Keeping the racket out in front on the volley.
- Quick volley reflexes.
- Control of volleys.

PROCEDURE

- Players are divided into pairs, one player backed up against the fence facing the court, the other several feet away (or on the baseline) facing his or her partner at the fence.

SEQUENCE

- Player facing the fence starts the ball into play by volleying to partner.
- Partner volleys the ball back and players rally, volley-to-volley, trying to keep one ball in play as long as possible.
- When one player misses, either player starts a new ball into play immediately and the rally continues as before.
- After a specified period of time, players change partners by rotating one position clockwise.
- Repeat the same sequence until every player has rallied with every other player and everyone has had a turn against the fence.

FOR VARIETY

- Both players hit forehands or backhands only.
- One player hits forehands; the other hits backhands.
- Each player alternates — one forehand, then one backhand.

VOLLEYS

Hot Volleys

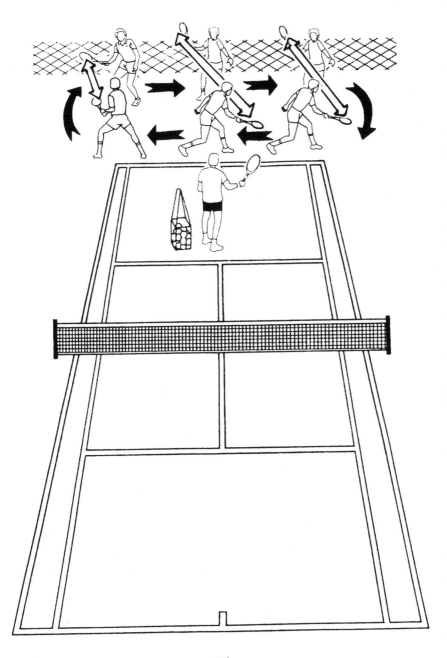

- Closing in from the service line.
- Control and placement of wide-reaching volleys.

PROCEDURE

- Players are lined up behind the service line along the ad court sideline.
- Pro feeds from across the net at the center of the service line.
- Target is located in the deep corner of the pro's ad court.

SEQUENCE

- Pro feeds first ball up the middle to player's forehand.
- First player in line moves to the right and hits forehand volley from near the service line, aiming for target, then closes in.
- Pro feeds second ball wide to the player's forehand.
- Player reacts to the direction of the ball and hits forehand volley down the line to target.
- Player rotates to the end of the line and the next player in line repeats the same sequence.

FOR VARIETY

- Reverse: To develop consistency and contol on both forehand and backhand reaching volleys, repeat the same two-volley sequence in reverse. Players will line up on the opposite side of the court and hit backhand volleys instead of forehands, aiming for target placed deep in the corner of the deuce court.

German Volley Drill

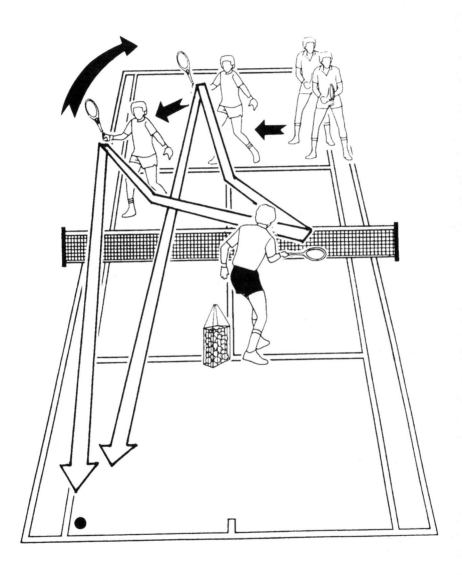

SKILL OBJECTIVES

- Short angle volleys.
- Footwork and movement.

PROCEDURE

- Players line up in two lines along the singles sidelines behind the service line.
- The first player in each line is the volleyer. Other players shadow the motions of the volleyers.
- Pro feeds from across the net, halfway between the service line and net on the center line.
- Targets are located on the singles sidelines, to the right and left of the pro, halfway between the service line and net.

SEQUENCE

- Pro feeds crosscourt to deuce court volleyer.
- Volleyer moves in and hits short angle volley crosscourt, aiming for deuce court target.
- Volleyer then side-hops back to starting position and waits in ready position, keeping the feet moving all the while.
- Pro feeds to ad court volleyer.
- Volleyer moves in, hits short angle volley crosscourt to ad court target, side-hops back to starting position, and keeps feet moving while waiting for the next feed.
- Repeat the same sequence for a total of 10 feeds to each of the two volleyers.
- After 10 hits each, players rotate to the end of the opposite line.

FOR VARIETY

- Two players pick up balls during each rotation.

78

Shadow
Short Angle Volley

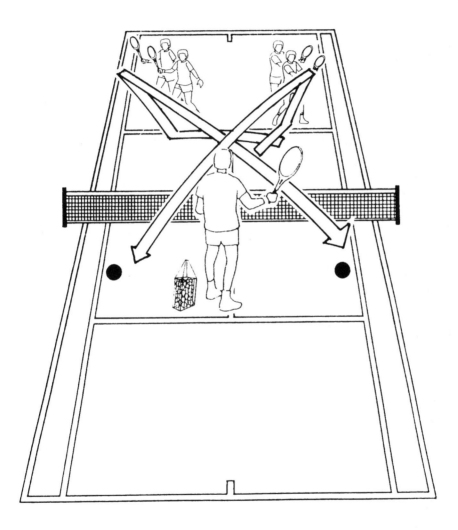

SKILL OBJECTIVES

- Split step.
- Poaching volley.
- Closing volley.

PROCEDURE

- Players line up behind ad court service line.
- Pro feeds from across the net, from the backhand corner of the deuce court service block.
- One target is placed at the intersection of the service line and center line.
- The other target is placed halfway between the service line and net on the singles sideline of the pro's ad court.

SEQUENCE

- As the pro drops the ball to feed, the first player in line takes one step forward and splits.
- Pro feeds to the player's forehand or backhand.
- Player closes in and volleys down the line to the pro.
- Pro volleys (or feeds next ball) crosscourt.
- Player poaches and volleys up the middle or short angle to the sideline, aiming for target.
- Player goes to the end of the line.
- Repeat same sequence with next player in line.

FOR VARIETY

- Feed the second ball as a lob instead of a volley. Poaching player must run down the lob or play overhead out of the air.
- Put one player in hot seat next to pro to attempt to return balls when player poaches.
- Have one player go to pick up balls during each rotation.

Volley Poach Drill

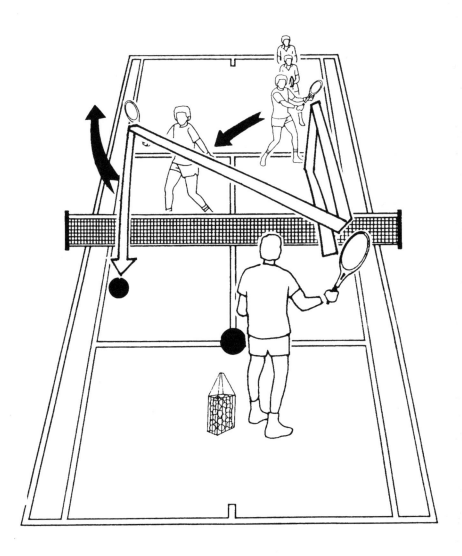

SKILL OBJECTIVES

- Cut off angle of opponent's return.
- Quick footwork and recovery.
- Racket control and direction of placement.

PROCEDURE

- Targets are placed 2' inside singles sideline at service line.
- Players are lined up in two lines on the other side of the net along the center service line.
- First player in each line is the volleyer.
- Other players shadow the motions of the volleyer at the head of the line.
- Pro feeds from center of service line.

SEQUENCE

- Pro feeds toward deuce court alley.
- Volleyer A closes in using quick small steps, hits short angle volley toward ad court target, then recovers by side-hopping back to starting position.
- Pro feeds toward ad court alley.
- Volleyer B closes in, volleys toward deuce court target, and recovers starting position.
- Repeat same sequence for a total of 10 shots for each of the first two volleyers.
- Volleyer A goes to the end of line B and Volleyer B goes to the end of line A.
- Repeat the same sequence with the next two players at the head of each line, for a total of 10 shots each, and continue in the same pattern as players rotate through the lines.

FOR VARIETY

- Players volley to crosscourt target.
- Players go to pick up balls after 10 shots.

Closing Volley

SKILL OBJECTIVES

- Timing the poach.
- Keeping the volley deep.

PROCEDURE

- Pro feeds from the middle of the ad court service line.
- Receivers are lined up one behind the other at the middle of the deuce court on the baseline opposite the pro.
- Poachers are lined up in two lines on either side of the pro, one line in the alley, the other along the center line, halfway between the service line and net.

SEQUENCE

- Pro feeds down the line to the receiver.
- Receiver returns the ball down the line.
- Poacher from alley line poaches diagonally and hits forehand volley down the line.
- Next receiver hits down the line.
- Poacher from center line poaches diagonally and hits backhand volley down the line.
- Drill continues in the same pattern as receivers rotate among themselves and poachers rotate lines.
- Players try to keep one ball in play for 20 to 30 hits without the pro having to introduce a new feed.

FOR VARIETY

- Receivers rotate to become poachers and poachers go to the other end to become receivers.
- Receivers move in to the service line and volley the ball back down the line.
- Poachers volley crosscourt to put the ball away.

84

Japanese
Poaching Drill

SKILL OBJECTIVES

- Angle volleys used in doubles play.
- Racket control for accuracy of placement.
- Hit-and-recovery footwork at the net.

PROCEDURE

- Players are lined up in two lines, one on each singles sideline, halfway between the service line and net.
- The player at the head of each line is the volleyer. Other players shadow the motions of the volleyers.
- Pro feeds from the center of the service line across the net.
- Targets are placed in the deep corners of the deuce and ad court service blocks, next to the sidelines to the pro's right and left.

SEQUENCE

- Pro feeds the ball up the middle to Volleyer A.
- Volleyer A closes in using small quick steps, hits angle volley to deuce court target, and recovers by side-hopping back to the starting position.
- Pro feeds up the middle to Volleyer B.
- Volleyer B closes in, volleys to ad court target, and recovers to starting position.
- After 10 hits each, Volleyer A goes to the end of line B and Volleyer B goes to the end of line A.

FOR VARIETY

- Volleyers close in on same angle but player A hits to ad court target and Volleyer B hits to deuce court target.
- Volleyers go to pick up balls after 10 hits each.
- Move targets in halfway to the net to sharpen the angle.

Doubles Closing Volley

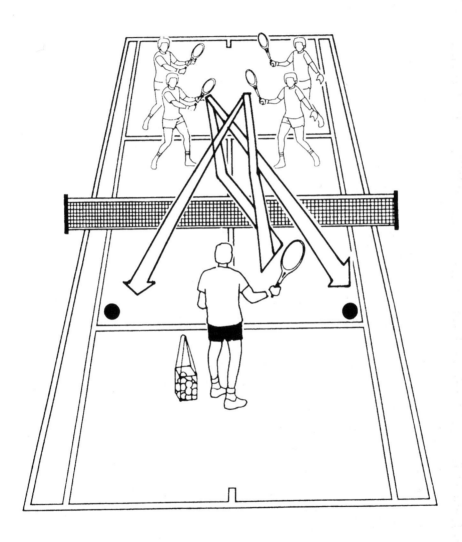

SKILL OBJECTIVES

- Footwork and movement.
- Control and placement of groundstrokes and volleys.

PROCEDURE

- Players are divided into two groups, one group on each end of the court.
- Groundstrokers are lined up behind the center of the baseline.
- Pro feeds from behind the center of the opposite service line.
- Volleyers are lined up on the pro's end of the court, outside the ad court alley, halfway between the service line and net.

SEQUENCE

- Pro feeds first ball deep into deuce court.
- First volleyer in line moves into net position in the pro's ad court.
- First groundstroker in line moves to the right and hits forehand groundstroke down the line.
- Volleyer returns the ball down the line with a backhand volley, then recovers.
- Pro feeds second ball deep into ad court.
- Groundstroker moves wide to the left and hits backhand groundstroke down the line.
- Volleyer moves across to cut off the ball and hits forehand volley back down the line.
- Repeat the same sequence for a total of two hits by each player.
- Players rotate and the next two players repeat the sequence.

FOR VARIETY

- Players hit crosscourt instead of down the line.

Groundstroke
and Volley

SKILL OBJECTIVES

- Down-the-line passing shots.
- Split step and closing volley.
- Short angle volleys.

PROCEDURE

- Groundstrokers start at center of baseline.
- Players lined up behind groundstrokers shadow the exact motion of the groundstrokers.
- Volleyers are positioned across the net on the service line.
- Pro feeds from center service line on the same side of the net as the volleyers.
- Targets are placed on singles sideline at service line.

SEQUENCE

- Pro feeds ball to corner of deuce court.
- Volleyer A closes in toward the net.
- Groundstroker A moves to the right to hit passing shot down the line.
- Volleyer A closes in, takes split step as groundstroker prepares to hit and volleys short angle crosscourt to target.
- Groundstroker side-hops back to starting position at center of baseline and goes to the end of line B.
- Repeat same procedure, this time feeding to Groundstroker B on the ad court side.
- Players rotate positions as the drill continues.

FOR VARIETY

- Have one or two players pick up balls during each rotation.

Passing Shot
and Volley

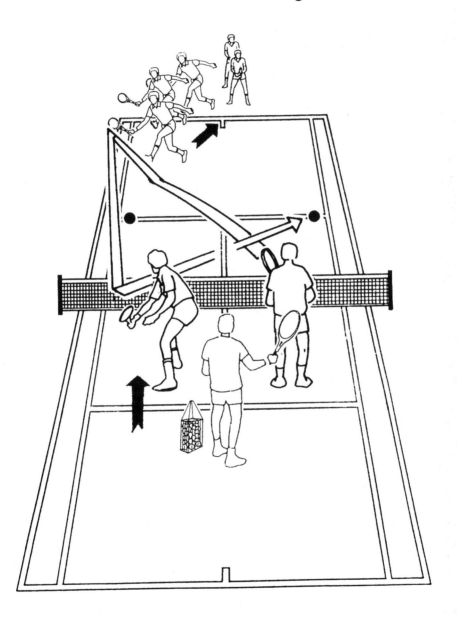

SKILL OBJECTIVES

- Crosscourt passing shots under pressure.
- Movement in the direction of the ball.
- Closing volleys.

PROCEDURE

- Groundstrokers start at center of baseline.
- Pro feeds from center of service line across the net.
- Volleyers start on the pro's service line.

SEQUENCE

- Pro feeds to deuce court.
- Volleyers close in toward the net, moving in the same direction as the ball, then split.
- Groundstroker moves to the right and hits crosscourt passing shot.
- Volleyer intercepts passing shot and hits short angle volley into opponent's ad court alley.
- Players side-hop back to starting position.
- Repeat the same sequence, this time feeding to the ad court. The closing volley will be aimed into the deuce court alley.
- Players rotate.

FOR VARIETY

- Have one or two players go to pick up balls during each rotation.

Passing and Closing

SKILL OBJECTIVES

- Consistency and placement of half-volleys.
- Half-volley preparation, moving from side to side.

PROCEDURE

- Player starts at the center of the service line.
- Pro feeds from across the net at the center of the baseline.

SEQUENCE

- Pro feeds into the deuce court service block.
- Player moves to the right and plays half-volley down the line.
- Pro feeds into ad court service block.
- Player moves to the left and hits half-volley down the line.
- Repeat the same sequence, alternating feeds from one side to the other, until players master the timing of the stroke, moving from side to side, and placing the ball consistently down the line on both the forehand and backhand sides.

FOR VARIETY

- Provide targets for down-the-line placement.
- When working with more than one player, other players may line up behind the hitter to shadow the hitter's motions. One player goes to pick up balls as players rotate after a desired number of hits.

Half Volley
for Depth

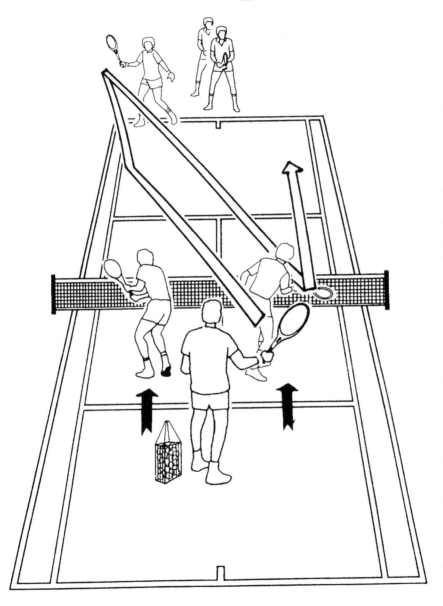

Lobs

SKILL OBJECTIVES

- Offensive and defensive lobs.
- Lobbing over the opponent at the net.

PROCEDURE

- Players are lined up behind the center of the baseline.
- Pro feeds from across the net at the center of the service line.
- Target is located in the deep corner of the pro's deuce court.

SEQUENCE

- Pro feeds ball deep and wide to the deuce court.
- First player in line runs wide and hits high lob over the pro's head, aiming for target. (If the lob is not enough to clear the pro's reach, pro returns the ball and the player lobs again. Each player gets nine chances to "clear the pro.")
- Player then rotates to the end of the line and the next player in line becomes the hitter.

FOR VARIETY

- Each player receives two feeds. Player hits forehand groundstroke crosscourt then lobs the second ball.
- Reverse: Repeat the same drill on the backhand side.
- Experienced players practice topspin lobs.

Clear the Pro

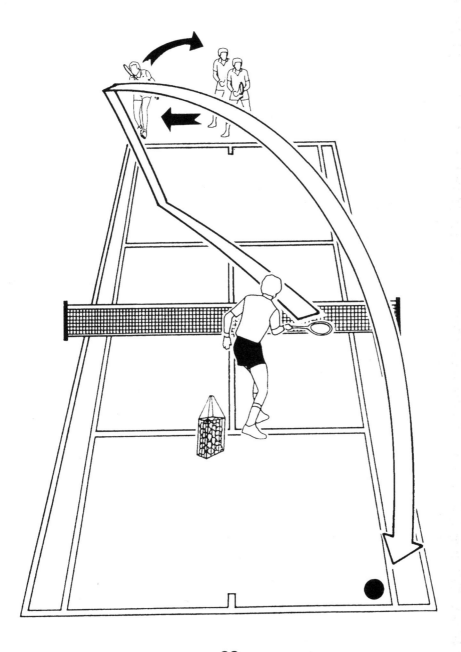

SKILL OBJECTIVES

- Consistency in executing topspin lobs.
- Using the topspin lob as an offensive tactic.

PROCEDURE

- Hitter is on the service line behind the deuce or ad court service block.
- Feeder is directly across the net from one hitter, on the opposite service line.
- Other players are lined up in the alley near the hitter.
- Ball basket is located at the center of feeder's service line.

SEQUENCE

- Feeder feeds the ball across the net with a drop-and-hit into the hitter's service block.
- Hitter plays a topspin lob over the feeder's head. WHEN EXECUTING THE TOPSPIN LOB, THE FOLLOW-THROUGH ENDS WITH THE RACKET OVER THE SHOULDER OF THE HITTING ARM.
- Repeat for a total of four hits.
- Players rotate: Hitter rotates to become the new feeder, feeder goes to the end of the line, and the first player in line in the alley is a new hitter.
- The sequence is repeated and players continue to rotate after four hits each.

FOR VARIETY

- Feeder may attempt to retrieve the topspin lob after it has bounced and players play out the point, using only half the width of the court.
- Hitters move back to 3/4 court, then to the baseline.

Topspin Lobs

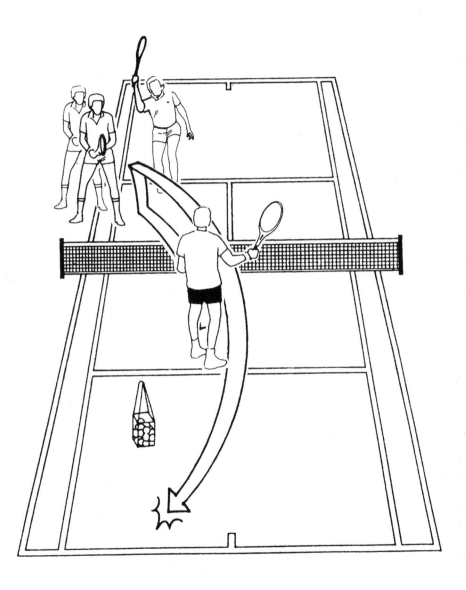

The Overhead

SKILL OBJECTIVES

- Overhead smash out of the air.
- Footwork for proper positioning for overheads.
- Defending against the lob.

PROCEDURE

- Players line up in starting position at the center of the baseline.
- Pro feeds from the opposite baseline.

SEQUENCE

- First player in line runs in and touches the net with his or her racket.
- Pro feeds lob.
- Player backs up and plays overhead smash out of the air then returns to end of line.
- As the first player hits, the next player in line runs in and touches net with racket.
- Pro feeds lob.
- Player backs up, hits overhead smash out of the air, and returns to end of line.
- The same sequence is repeated as players continue to rotate after one hit each.

FOR VARIETY

- For less experienced players, have the players line up at the service line instead of the baseline.
- As the players' skill level progresses, more challenging feeds can be introduced, requiring the players to choose whether to play the ball out of the air or turn and run down the lob and play the ball back after it has bounced.

Overhead Smash

SKILL OBJECTIVES

- Proper positioning and footwork on the overhead.
- Feeling the motion and visualizing the kill.

PROCEDURE

- Hitter is in the deuce court service block, halfway between the net and service line.
- Shadows are lined up side-by-side to the left of the hitter to shadow the motions of the hitter.
- Pro feeds from the baseline directly opposite the hitter.
- Target is located in the deep corner of the pro's deuce court.

SEQUENCE

- Pro feeds lob (drop-and-hit) to the hitter.
- Hitter turns and prepares racket, adjusts feet for proper positioning, and hits overhead smash crosscourt to target.
- Shadows should concentrate on turning the body sideways, adjusting the feet, and reaching up to swing.
- After three hits, players rotate to their right and the same sequence continues.

FOR VARIETY

- Move the target to the ad court corner. Pro feeds from deuce court to player nearest the ad court sideline. Players hit backhand overheads crosscourt to ad court target and rotate to the left after three hits each.

Shadow Overhead

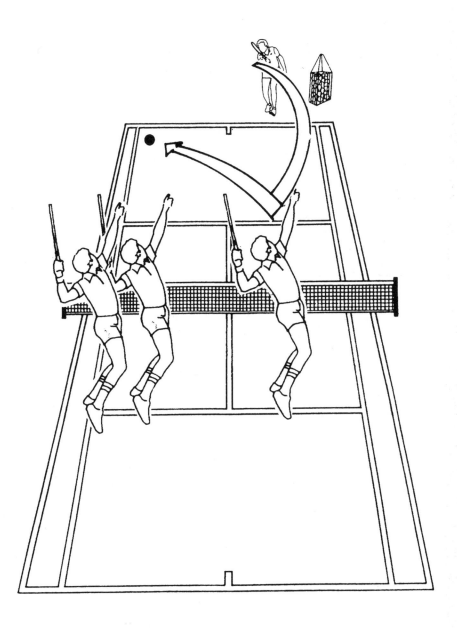

SKILL OBJECTIVES

- Footwork for proper positioning on the overhead.
- Racket control and preparation.
- Placement of overheads hit out of the air.

PROCEDURE

- Players are lined up across the width of the court, halfway between the service line and net on one end of the court—one player in each service block, one in each alley, and one on either side outside the doubles alley.
- Players in the service blocks are the hitters.
- Players in the alley shadow the hitters' motion.
- Players outside the alley are jogging in place.
- Pro feeds from the center of the baseline to the opposite end of the court.
- Targets are placed in the deep corners of the pro's deuce and ad courts.

SEQUENCE (As one hitter hits, the other runs in to touch the net with his or her racket.)

- Pro feeds lob to ad court hitters.
- Hitter backs up and hits overhead out of the air to deuce court target, then runs in again.
- Pro feeds lob to deuce court hitter.
- Hitter backs up, hits overhead out of the air to ad court target, then runs in again.
- Repeat for a total of two hits each.
- Players rotate: Hitters run back to the fence, then rotate to the opposite sides of the court to jog in place. Joggers become shadows, and shadows move into position to become hitters.

Footrace to Overhead

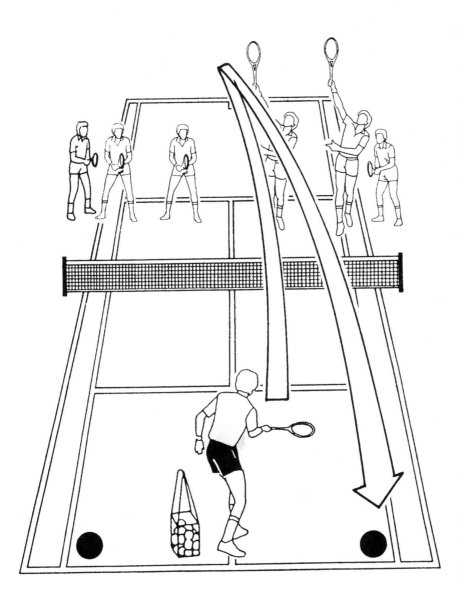

Munchkin Drills

SKILL OBJECTIVES

- Hand-eye coordination.
- Control over the direction of the ball with the racket.

PROCEDURE

- Players are divided into two teams with an equal number of players on each team.
- With one team on each end of the court, players line up behind the service line at the singles sideline. One team competes against the other.
- Players must dribble the ball on the court with their racket as they run.
- The first player on each team starts at the same time. When one player reaches the baseline, the next player in line on that team begins.

SEQUENCE

- Dribbling the ball with the racket, each team member runs:
- Down the sideline to the net,
- Back to the service line,
- Across to the center line,
- Down the center line to the net,
- Back to the service line,
- Across to the far singles sideline,
- Down the sideline to the net,
- Up the alley to the baseline,
  (The first **TEAM** to finish wins the race).

FOR VARIETY

- Players dribble the ball up in the air off their racket instead of down on the ground.
- Each time players change directions they change the dribble from up in the air to down on the ground.

Dribble Race

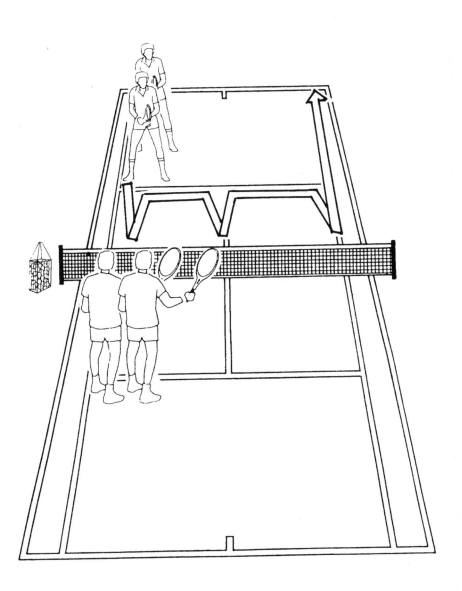

SKILL OBJECTIVES

- Movement.
- Control of depth and direction.
- Concentration.

PROCEDURE

- Players are divided into four groups.
- Each group lines up behind the service line, one group behind each service block.

SEQUENCE

- Players in the deuce court rally with players in the opposite deuce court.
- Players in the ad court rally with players in the opposite ad court.
- Each player hits one groundstroke into the diagonally opposite service court, then rotates to the end of the line.
- Players attempt to keep the crosscourt rally going without a miss as players continue to rotate after one hit each.

FOR VARIETY

- Deuce court players compete against ad court players to see which team can rally the most hits without missing.
- Deuce court players hit only forehands. Ad court players hit only backhands. Each miss scores one point for the opposing team and teams compete to win seven points. Players change sides after one team scores seven points.

Crosscourt
Mini-Tennis

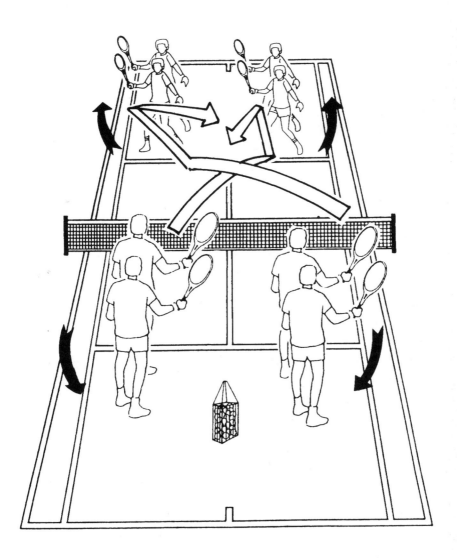

SKILL OBJECTIVES

- Control of ball depth and speed.
- Anticipation
- Concentration.

PROCEDURE

- 4-8 players on each end of the court are lined up behind the center of the service line.

SEQUENCE

- The first player in line on one team feeds the ball with a groundstroke hit inside the service line to the first player on the opposing team.
- Hitter rotates to the end of the line.
- Opponent returns a groundstroke within the service court and rotates to the end of the line.
- Players from each team continue to rally groundstroke-to-groundstroke, rotating after each hit, until one player misses.
- Each miss scores one point for the opposing team. The first team to score 11 points wins.

FOR VARIETY

- Use only half the width of the court.
- Players hit only forehands.
- Players hit only backhands.
- Players on one team hit forehands, the other team hits backhands. Switch after one team scores 11 points.

Ping-Pong
Mini-Tennis

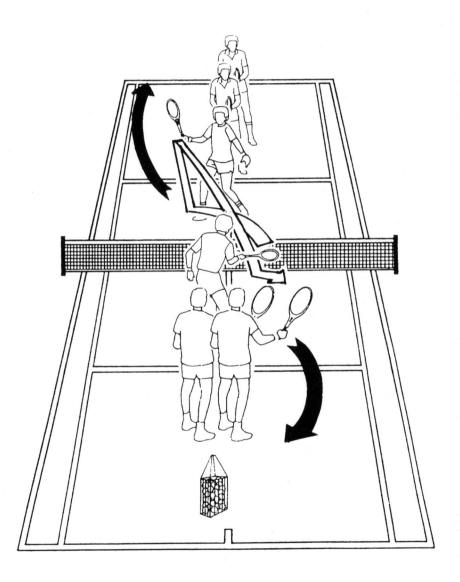

SKILL OBJECTIVES

- Movement for proper positioning of groundstrokes.
- Control of ball speed and depth.

PROCEDURE

- Players are lined up in two lines, one line on each end of the court behind the center of the service line.

SEQUENCE

- The first player in line on one end of the court starts the ball into play with a groundstroke inside the opponent's service line.
- The hitter then runs to the end of the opposite line.
- The opponent returns the ball with a groundstroke across the net into the service court, then runs to the end of the opposite line.
- Next player in line returns the ball and players continue to rally, rotating to the end of the opposite line after one hit each, until someone misses.
- When someone misses, the player who has missed drops out.
- Players repeat the sequence until only two players remain.
- The last two players do not rotate but rally out the point until one player wins.

FOR VARIETY

- Use only half the width of the court.
- Players hit only forehands from one end of the court and only backhands from the other.

118

Around the World Mini-Tennis

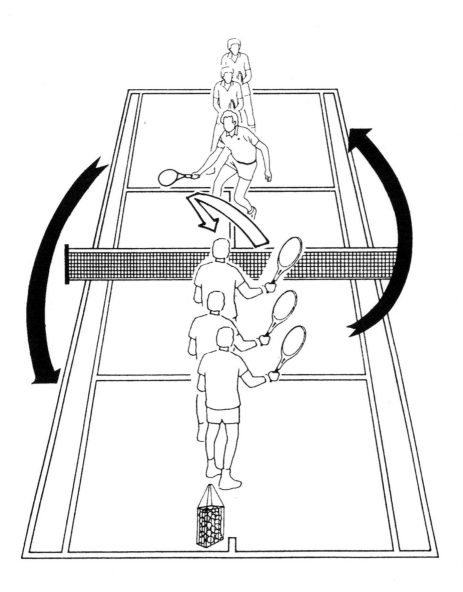

Singles Match-Play Tactics

SKILL OBJECTIVES

- Consistency and placement of groundstrokes.
- Hitting for depth.

PROCEDURE

- Two players are in serving position at the baseline of one end of the court, one on the deuce side and one on the ad side.
- Two players are in position to receive serve at the opposite end of the court, one on the deuce side and one on the ad side.
- Two players wait behind the servers to rotate in.
- Ballbasket is located behind the baseline between the two servers.

SEQUENCE

- Both servers serve at the same time to their respective receivers.
- Receivers return the ball crosscourt and players rally groundstrokes crosscourt for a maximum of 10 hits. GROUNDSTROKES ONLY. NO LOBS ALLOWED. ALL SHOTS MUST LAND BEHIND THE SERVICE LINE. BALL MUST BE HIT AFTER ONE BOUNCE ONLY.
- Servers alternate with players waiting to rotate in after one serve each.
- After 10 serves and returns, players rotate. Servers become receivers and vice versa.

FOR VARIETY

- Doubles alley may be used in rallying.
- Players hit only forehands or only backhands.
- Players rally down the line instead of crosscourt.
- Servers compete against receivers for 11-, 15-, or 21-point games.

Singles Depth
Control Rally

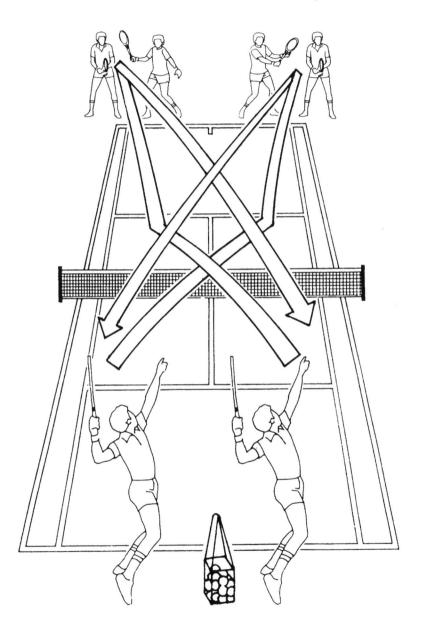

SKILL OBJECTIVES

- Quick movement up and back.
- Closing in to retrieve drop shots.
- Placing retrieved drop shots to keep the opponent on the defensive.

PROCEDURE

- Feeder starts on the service line on one side (deuce or ad side) of the court.
- Opponent is on the opposite service line, directly across the net from the feeder.
- Other players are lined up in the alley near the feeder.
- Ball basket is located at the center of the feeder's service line.

SEQUENCE

- Feeder feeds the ball across the net into the opponent's service block, then runs back and touches the baseline with his or her racket.
- Opponent returns the ball with a drop shot into the feeder's service block.
- Feeder runs in from the baseline to retrieve the drop shot and the two players play out the point using only half the width of the court.
- Players rotate: First player in line in the alley becomes the new feeder, opponent rotates to the end of the line, and the player who was the feeder becomes the new opponent.
- The same sequence is repeated as players continue to rotate after each point.

FOR VARIETY

- With four or more players per court, players may be divided into two groups, with one group executing the drill on each half of the width of the court.

124

Drop Shot Drill

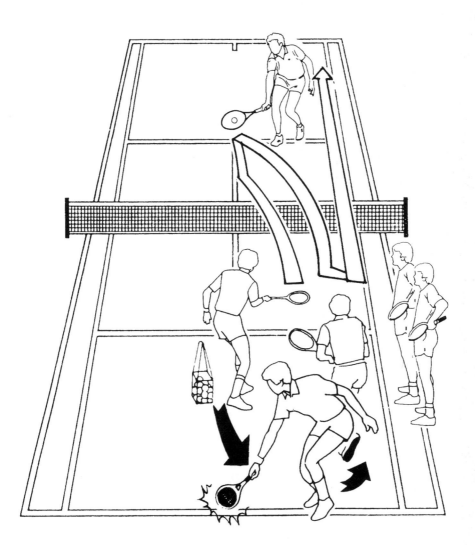

SKILL OBJECTIVES

- Control and consistency of groundstrokes.
- Hitting for depth.
- Moving in relation to the ball in singles.

PROCEDURE

- All three players start on the baseline, two on one end and one on the other.
- Play is confined to the singles court.

SEQUENCE

- Singles player starts the ball into play with a drop-and-hit to the deuce court player on the opposite baseline.
- Deuce court player hits groundstroke back to singles player.
- Singles player hits groundstroke back across the net to the ad court player.
- Ad court player returns groundstroke to singles player and the point begins.
- Players play out the point, 2-on-l, within the singles court.

FOR VARIETY

- Singles player puts the ball into play by serving, first to the deuce court, then to the ad court, as in regular match play.
- Players may close in to the net after the third hit.
- Players may close in to the net on any ball which lands inside the service line.

Two-on-One Singles

SKILL OBJECTIVES

- Quick concentration ability.
- Motivation to keep the ball in play.

PROCEDURE

- Two or three players line up on each end of the court to play as a team.
- One player from each team plays at a time.
- One end of the court is designated as the "feed end".
- Play is confined to the singles court.

SEQUENCE

- The first player on the "feed end" feeds the ball to the opponent to put the ball into play and begin the point.
- Players play out the point.
- The winner of the point stays in to play the next point. The loser is relieved by a teammate before the next point begins.
- Play continues until one team has scored 11 or 21 points.

FOR VARIETY

- Alternate "feed end" so that the teams take turns putting the ball into play.
- Rotate individual players to make up new teams or to even up the teams.

SINGLES MATCH-PLAY TACTICS

Team Tennis Singles

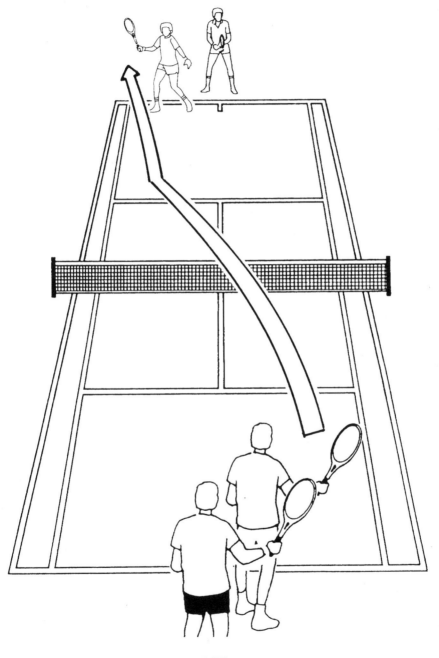

SKILL OBJECTIVES

- Defending against the opponent at the net.
- Lobbing the opponent at the net.
- Passing with a hook shot.
- Returning the drop shot.

PROCEDURE

- Players are divided into two teams. One team lines up behind the baseline on the ad side of the court. The other team lines up behind the opposite baseline on the deuce side.
- Pro feeds from outside the alley near the net, on the side of the court nearest the players.

SEQUENCE

- Pro feeds drop shot across the net.
- First player in line on the receiving team runs in and plays drop shot in return.
- First player on opposing team runs in from the baseline and attempts to win the point with either a topspin lob over the opponent's head or a hook shot angled crosscourt for a passing shot winner.

(The "hook shot" is executed with the same motion as a topspin lob but the racket is kept a bit more on edge, with less of an open face, and the ball is angled sharply crosscourt.)

- Each point is played out until one player hits a clear winner, scoring one point for his or her team.
- The same sequence is repeated with the next two players in line becoming the hitters, as the first two hitters return to the end of the line.
- Teams compete for the best of three sets, 10 points per set, with each team receiving five feeds per set.

Lob-Hook Shot Option

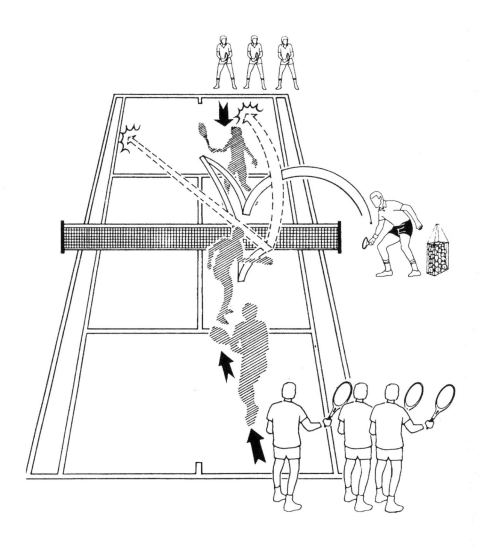

SKILL OBJECTIVES

- Quick movement at the net.
- Fast feet and controlled racket.

PROCEDURE

- Players line up in starting position at the center of the baseline.
- Pro feeds from opposite end of the court at the center of the baseline.
- Targets are placed deep in the pro's court near the singles sidelines.

SEQUENCE

- Pro feeds three-ball sequence to each hitter:
  - (1) low to the forehand
  - (2) wide to the backhand
  - (3) lob
- Hitter aims for targets as follows:
  - (1) forehand crosscourt
  - (2) backhand crosscourt
  - (3) overhead smash to ad court target
- Hitter goes to the end of the line.

FOR VARIETY

- If all shots are "in," player goes to the end of the line. If any shot is "out," player must pick up 10 balls and rush to get back in line before his or her next turn.
- Players score points for hitting targets.

Go For It

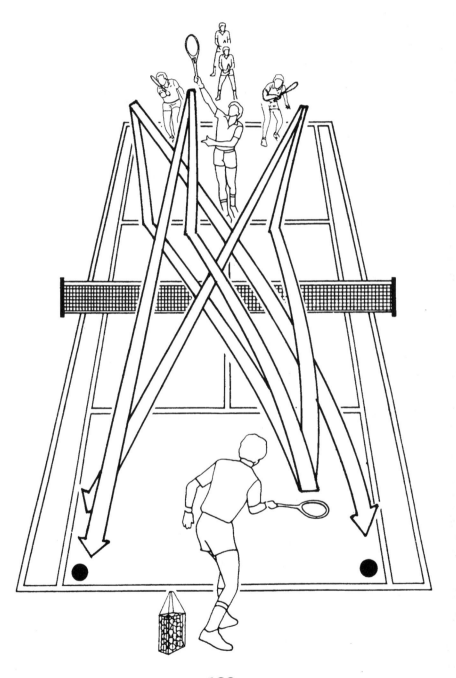

SKILL OBJECTIVES

- Singles movement.
- Down-the-line groundstrokes and volleys.
- Closing in to net.
- Closing out the point.

PROCEDURE

- Hitters line up at the center of the baseline.
- Pro feeds from across the net halfway between the baseline and center service line.
- Targets are placed in the far corners of the pro's court near the baseline and singles sidelines.

SEQUENCE

- Pro feeds a five-ball sequence to each hitter in turn. The hitter aims all shots down the line at targets, as follows:
  (1) forehand groundstroke
  (2) backhand groundstroke
  (3) forehand approach shot
  (4) backhand volley
  (5) overhead smash to ad court target to close out the point.
- Hitter goes to pick up balls before returning to the end of the line.
- Pro feeds same sequence of shots to next hitter in line.

Cover the Court

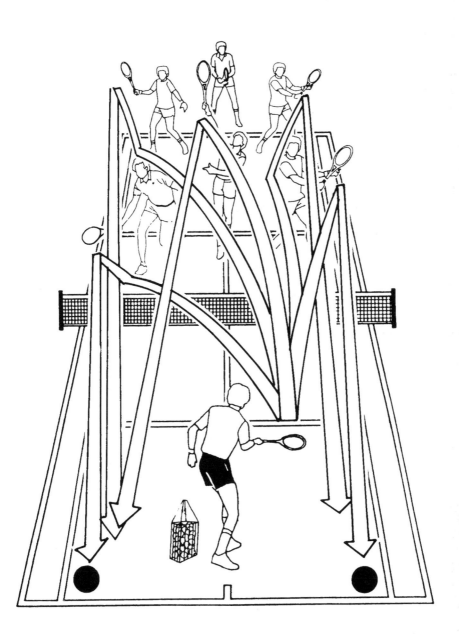

SKILL OBJECTIVES

- Passing shots.
- Putting away short returns
- Movement.

PROCEDURE

- Players line up in starting position at the center of the baseline.
- Pro feeds from the center of the deuce court service block across the net.

SEQUENCE

- Pro feeds down the line into player's ad court.
- Player moves left and hits down the line back to the pro.
- Pro volleys (or feeds) short ball crosscourt.
- Player moves in and hits "kill shot" down the line to put the ball away.

FOR VARIETY

- Reverse: Feed first ball to player's forehand.

  Feed short ball to backhand.
  a. Player hits aggressive shot down the line for a winner.
  b. Player hits kill shot crosscourt.

Passing Shot and Kill Shot

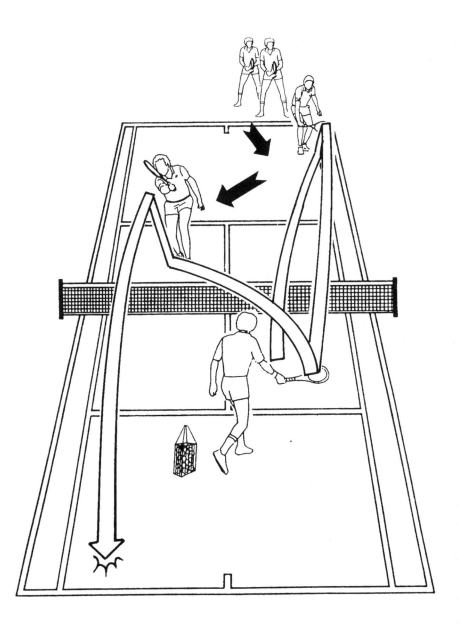

SKILL OBJECTIVES

- Passing shots.
- Putting away short returns
- Hitting on the move.

PROCEDURE

- Players line up in starting position at the center of the baseline.
- Pro feeds from the center of the deuce court service block across the net.

SEQUENCE

- Pro feeds crosscourt to player's forehand.
- Player moves to the right and returns the ball to the pro.
- Pro volleys (or feeds) down the line.
- Player moves to the left and hits the ball back down the line to the pro.
- Pro volleys (or feeds) short ball crosscourt.
- Player moves in and hits "kill shot" down the line to put the ball away.

FOR VARIETY

- Place targets 3' inside the baseline near singles sidelines. Players aim for the target on the "kill shot".
- Reverse the drill: Feed first ball to player's backhand, second to forehand, and short ball to backhand. Player will aim "kill shot" at crosscourt target or go for backhand "kill shot" down the line for a winner.

Three-Ball Putaway

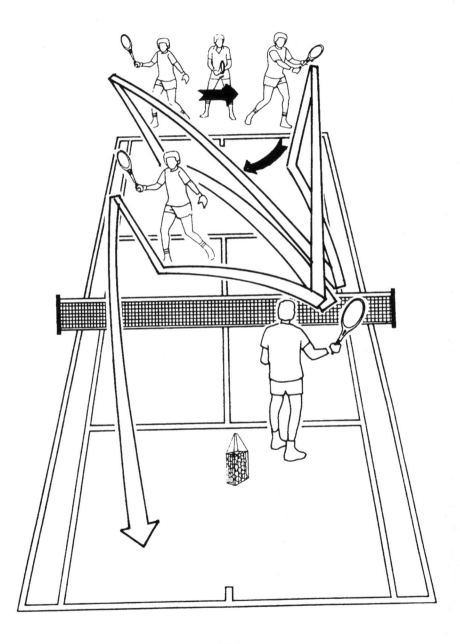

SKILL OBJECTIVES

- Closing in behind the serve.
- Split step and volley.

PROCEDURE

- Server is in position to serve from the deuce court.
- Shadow is next to the server, on the server's right.
- Pro is in position to receive serve from the deuce court.

SEQUENCE

- Server serves to pro.
- Shadow imitates service motion, closes in, and takes split step as pro prepares to hit.
- Pro hits return of serve crosscourt.
- Shadow volleys the ball down the line.
- Repeat for a specified number of serves.
- Players rotate.

FOR VARIETY

- Shadow volleys the ball crosscourt instead of down the line.
- Shadow closes in and hits two volleys, one crosscourt back to the pro, then the second one down the line to close out the point.

Serve and Volley

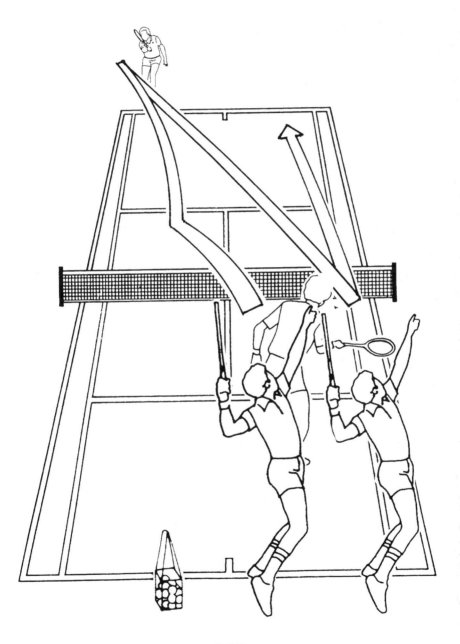

SKILL OBJECTIVES

- Using the forehand as an offensive weapon.
- Forcing the opponent deep.
- Putting the short ball away.

PROCEDURE

- Players are lined up behind the center of the baseline.
- Pro feeds from across the net at the center of the service line.
- Targets are located in the deep corners of the pro's ad and deuce court.

SEQUENCE

- Pro feeds short, high ball into deuce court.
- First player in line moves in and hits aggressive forehand shot down the line to ad court target.
  (Player should avoid the temptation to overhit the ball.)
- Pro feeds short, high ball into the ad court.
- Player runs around the backhand and uses the same aggressive forehand shot to hit down the line on the backhand side.
- Player rotates to the end of the line and the next player in line repeats the same sequence.

FOR VARIETY

- Player closes in after the second shot, pro feeds again to the backhand side, and player puts this third ball away with a forehand volley.

142

Step-Away Forehands

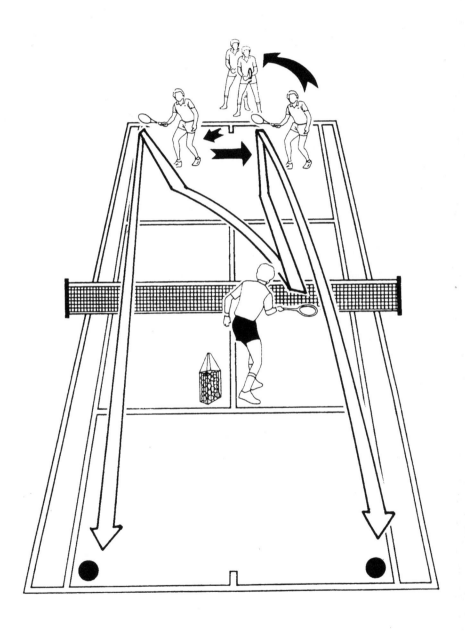

SKILL OBJECTIVES

- Consistency and placement of half-volleys and volleys.
- Quick footwork and reflexes at the net.
- Closing in and covering the line.

PROCEDURE

- Pro feeds from center of baseline.
- Volleyer starts at service line in pro's deuce court.
- Half-volleyer starts at center of service line across the net from the pro.

SEQUENCE

- Pro feeds into deuce court service block.
- Volleyer in pro's court moves to the left, moving "with the ball" to cover the open court.
- Half-volleyer moves to the right, plays half-volley down the line and closes in.
- Volleyer moves to cover the line and volleys the ball back down the line.
- Players play out the point, volley-to-volley down the line until one player forces the other to miss.

FOR VARIETY

- Reverse: Repeat the same sequence but this time feeding to the ad court. Half-volleyer will move left to cover the ad court line. Volleyer will move right, into the deuce court to cover the line.
- Players play a certain number of points from each side to develop consistency on both forehand and backhand volleys down the line. Players keep score and try to win.

Closing Down the Line

SKILL OBJECTIVES

- Moving laterally to the ball.
- Control and placement of passing shots.

PROCEDURE

- Players are lined up behind the baseline at the ad court singles sideline.
- Pro feeds from the center of the service line across the net.
- Target is located in the deep corner of the pro's ad court.

SEQUENCE

- Pro feeds deep ball up the middle.
- First player in line moves toward the center of the baseline and hits forehand groundstroke to ad court target.
- Pro feeds second ball deep and wide to the player's forehand.
- Player runs wide and hits forehand groundstroke down the line, aiming for target.
- Player rotates to the end of the line and the next player in line repeats the same two-shot sequence.

FOR VARIETY

- Use two targets and have players hit one shot crosscourt and the other down the line.
- Players hit both shots crosscourt, aiming for target placed in deep corner of deuce court.
- Reverse: Players repeat the same sequences from the opposite side of the court to hit backhands instead of forehands.

146

Covering
the Open Court

SKILL OBJECTIVES

- Serve and volley.
- Return of serve down the line.
- Crosscourt angle volley.

PROCEDURE

- Servers are in serving position behind the baseline of the deuce court.
- Receivers are in position to return serve from the opposite deuce court.

SEQUENCE

- Server serves wide to the forehand and closes in to net.
- Receiver hits return of serve down the line.
- Server hits backhand volley crosscourt for a winner.

FOR VARIETY

- With more than two players per court, other players line up and shadow the motions of the server and receiver. Players rotate after each turn.
- Reverse: Same alignment but this time players serve and return from the ad court. Servers serve wide to the backhand, receivers practice backhand returns down the line, and the server puts the ball away with a forehand volley angled crosscourt.

148

Serve and
Cover the Line

SKILL OBJECTIVES

- Serve and volley.
- Crosscourt return of serve.
- Volley for depth.

PROCEDURE

- Servers are in serving position behind baseline of deuce court.
- Receivers are in position to return serve from the opposite deuce court.

SEQUENCE

- Server serves wide to the forehand, closes in, and takes split step.
- Receiver hits return of serve crosscourt.
- Server volleys deep down the line for a winner.

FOR VARIETY

- With more than two players per court, other players line up and shadow the motions of the server and receiver. Players rotate after each turn. Server goes to receiving end. Receiver goes to serving end.
- Reverse: Same alignment but from the ad court side. Servers serve to backhand, receivers hit backhand returns crosscourt; servers hit backhand volleys down the line for winners.

Serve and
Cover the Angle

SKILL OBJECTIVES

- Closing in behind the serve.
- Consistency and control of volleys to set up the point.
- Closing out the point.

PROCEDURE

- Server is in position to serve from the deuce court.
- Receiver is in position to return serve from the opposite deuce court.

SEQUENCE

- Server serves wide to the receiver's forehand and closes in.
- Receiver hits offensive return of serve down the line.
- Server responds by hitting a firm volley back down the line, putting the receiver on the defensive.
- Receiver hits defensive shot down the line.
- Server volleys crosscourt to close out the point with a put-away volley.

FOR VARIETY

- Reverse: Repeat the same sequence from the ad court to develop consistency on both the forehand and backhand sides.
- With more than two players per court, others line up behind server and receiver to shadow their motions. Players rotate.

Set-up and Putaway

SKILL OBJECTIVES

- Passing shots with net person.
- Split step and closing volley.
- Short angle volleys.

PROCEDURE

- Groundstrokers start at center of baseline.
- Volleyers start at service line on opposite side of the net.
- Pro feeds from center service line on the same side of the net as the volleyers.
- Players behind groundstrokers shadow the exact motion of the groundstrokers.

SEQUENCE

- Pro feeds to far corner of deuce court.
- Volleyer on pro's ad court side closes in toward the net.
- Groundstroker moves to the right to play passing shot down the line.
- Volleyer split-steps and hits short angle volley into deuce court alley.
- Volleyer recovers starting position at service line and groundstroker side-hops back to center of baseline.
- Repeat same sequence, feeding to ad court side.
- Players rotate.

FOR VARIETY

- One or two players pick up balls during each rotation.

Pro's Pass and Volley

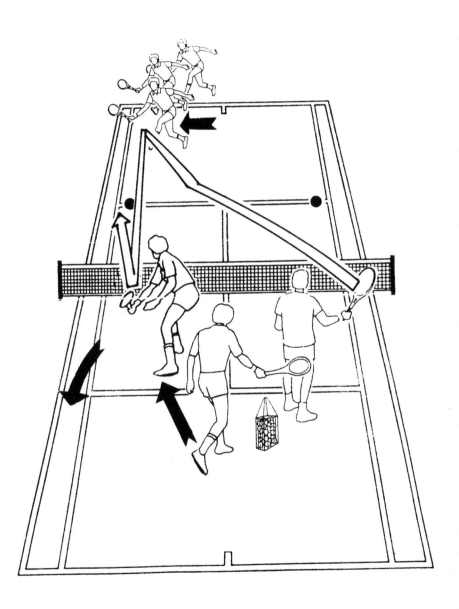

SKILL OBJECTIVES

- Consistency and placement of volleys and half-volleys.
- Offensive lobs and crosscourt angles.
- Quick reflexes at the net.

PROCEDURE

- Half-volleyer is in the ad court at the service line.
- Opponent is across the net at the service line of the deuce court.
- Pro feeds from near the baseline in the opponent's ad court.

SEQUENCE

- Pro feeds short ball crosscourt to half-volleyer.
- Half-volleyer places half-volley down the line to the opponent.
- Opponent returns the ball down the line.
- Half-volleyer either hits crosscourt angle or lobs over the opponent's head to win the point.
- Repeat same sequence for seven or 11 points, then players switch sides.

FOR VARIETY

- The opponent may attempt to save the point by covering the crosscourt angle or running down the lob. Play continues until the point is won or lost.
- Either player is allowed to try to win the point as soon as the possibility comes up.

Volley-Lob

SKILL OBJECTIVES

- Passing shots and volleys.
- Moving in relation to the ball.

PROCEDURE (3 players)

- One groundstroker is at the center of the baseline on one end of the court.
- Two volleyers are across the net, one in each service block.
- Pro feeds from the center on the service line behind the volleyers.

SEQUENCE

- Pro feeds deep ball up the middle to groundstroker.
- Groundstroker returns the ball to either volleyer and recovers.
- Volleyer returns the ball crosscourt or down the line within the singles lines.
- Groundstroker reacts to the direction of the ball, moves quickly into position to play the ball, and hits forehand or backhand either crosscourt or down the line in an attempt to pass the volleyers (within the doubles lines).
- Volleyers attempt to cut off the ball and the rally continues until the point is won, with the two volleyers competing as a team against the groundstroker. (NO LOBS ALLOWED.)
- Groundstroker scores two points (one bonus point) for each point won with a passing shot. Otherwise, players score one point for each miss by the opponent.
- After a period of time or a specified number of points won by either team, players rotate one position clockwise and play again.

Canadian Two-for-One

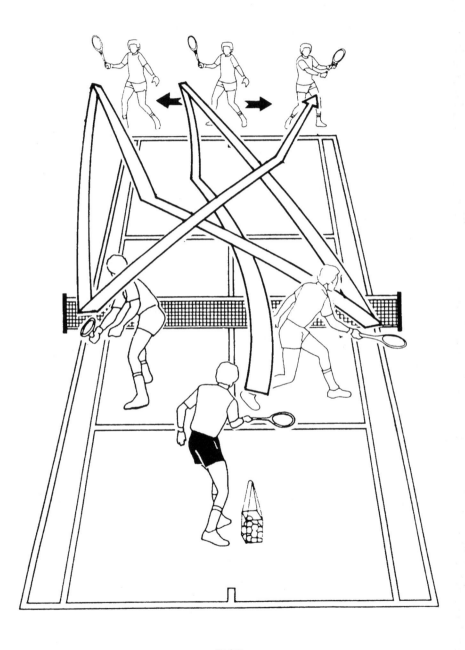

SKILL OBJECTIVES

- Moving laterally to the ball.
- Closing in on the short ball.
- Hitting the approach shot deep.

PROCEDURE

- Players are lined up behind the baseline at the ad court singles sideline.
- Pro feeds from the center of the service line across the net.
- Target is located in the deep corner of the pro's ad court.

SEQUENCE

- Pro feeds first ball deep up the middle.
- First player in line moves toward the center of the baseline and hits forehand groundstroke, aiming for target.
- Pro feeds second ball short to the deuce court.
- Player moves in and plays forehand approach shot down the line, going for depth, aiming for target.
- Player rotates to the end of the line and the next player in line repeats the same sequence.

FOR VARIETY

- Use two targets, one on each side of the court, deep in the corners. Players hit the first shot crosscourt to deuce court target, then approach down the line as before.
- Reverse: Players repeat the same sequence from the opposite side of the court to hit backhands instead of forehands.

Hit and Approach

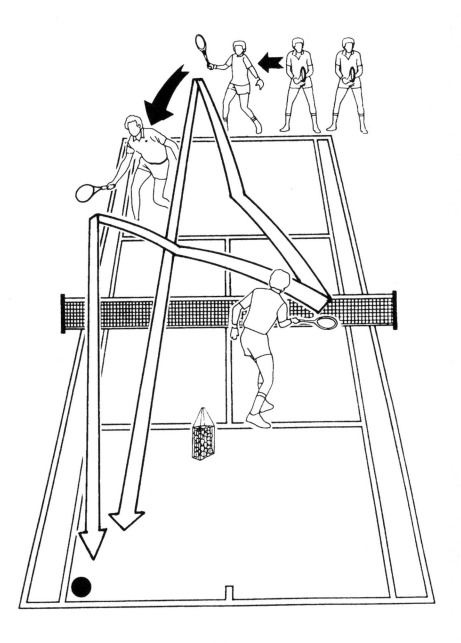

SKILL OBJECTIVES

- Forehand approach and putaway volley
- Backhand approach and putaway volley.

PROCEDURE

- Ball machine is located inside the baseline at the center of one end of the court.
- Ball machine is set to feed a short ball to the deuce court, then a short ball to the ad court, alternating from one side to the other continuously throughout the drill.
- Players form two lines at the baseline corners across the net from the ball machine.

SEQUENCE

- Ball machine feeds short ball to deuce court.
- First player in line on the deuce side of the court moves in, hits forehand approach shot down the line, and continues closing in to the net.
- Ball machine feeds short ball to ad court.
- First player in ad court line moves in, hits backhand approach shot down the line, then closes in to the net.
- Ball machine feeds short ball to deuce court.
- Deuce court player puts the ball away with a forehand volley then rotates to the end of the opposite line.
- Ball machine feeds to ad court.
- Ad court player puts the ball away with a backhand volley and rotates to the deuce court line.
- Next two players in line repeat the same sequence and the drill continues without interruption.

FOR VARIETY

- Pro feeds lob to each player after the player has hit the volley fed by the ball machine. Player hits overhead smash.

Approach and Volley

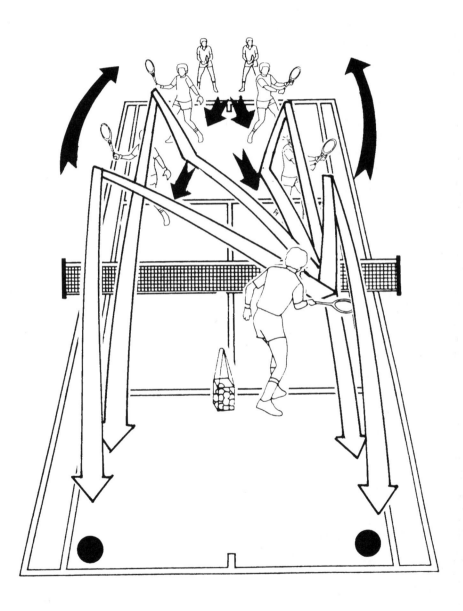

SKILL OBJECTIVES

- Approach shots down the line.
- Passing shots down the line.

PROCEDURE

- Players are divided into two groups, one group on each end of the court, lined up behind the baseline diagonally opposite each other on the deuce side of the court.

SEQUENCE

- First player in one line feeds short ball crosscourt to the opponent.
- Opponent moves in and hits forehand approach shot down the line.
- Feeder moves over to the ad court to cover the line and hits the ball back down the line.
- Players then play out the point, attempting to pass each other down the line, using only half the width of the court.
- Players rotate to the end of the line after playing out the point and the next two players in line repeat the same sequence.

FOR VARIETY

- Players are not allowed to use a lob in their attempt to win the point.
- Allow players to use the lob only after the first volley has been hit.
- Reverse: Repeat the same sequence from the ad side of the court so that the approach shot down the line will be played off the backhand.

164

Approach and Win

SKILL OBJECTIVES

- Control and placement of volleys.
- Setting up the winning volley.

PROCEDURE

- Server is at the service line, as if closing in behind the serve.
- Receiver is at the service line crosscourt from the server, near the sideline as if closing in behind a wide forehand return of serve.
- Pro feeds from midcourt position inside the receiver's baseline.

SEQUENCE

- Pro feeds a simulated return of serve to the server to start the ball into play.
- Server hits deep volley to receiver's forehand side, putting the receiver on the defensive.
- Receiver responds by hitting forehand volley down the line back to the server.
- Server covers the line and hits crisp backhand volley crosscourt for a winner.

FOR VARIETY

- Server and receiver start at the baseline. Server hits "fake serve" and closes in to start the drill. Receiver simulates the motion of returning serve as the pro feeds the first ball, then the drill continues as before.
- Reverse: Repeat the same sequence as if serving and receiving from the ad court.
- With more than two players per court, other players line up and shadow the motions of the hitters. Players rotate.

Set-up Volleys

SKILL OBJECTIVES

- Passing shots and volleys down the line.
- Forcing the weak return.
- Holding the line and closing out the point.

PROCEDURE

- Groundstroker starts at center of baseline.
- Volleyer is across the net on the ad court at the service line.
- Pro feeds from midcourt position on the same side of the net as the volleyer.

SEQUENCE

- Pro feeds wide ball crosscourt into the deuce court to the groundstroker.
- Groundstroker runs wide and returns the ball down the line.
- Volleyer volleys the ball back down the line.
- Groundstroker hits down the line again in an attempt to pass the volleyer.
- Volleyer "holds the line" if possible, hitting back down the line until a weak return by the groundstroker gives the volleyer an opportunity to put the ball away with a crosscourt angle volley.

FOR VARIETY

- Reverse: Repeat the same sequence from the opposite side of the court to develop consistent groundstrokes and volleys down the line on both the forehand and backhand sides.
- With more than two players per court, others line up and shadow the motions of the hitters. Players rotate after each turn.

Hold the Line

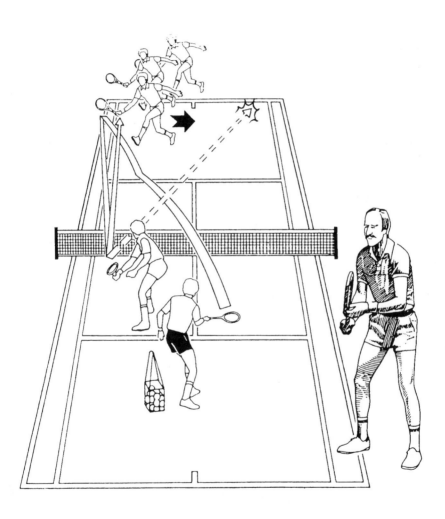

SKILL OBJECTIVES

- Control of volleys.
- Quick reflexes at the net.
- Passing the opponent at the net.

PROCEDURE

- A full court-length alley is marked off the center of the court, approximately the width of a service block. Use tape, chalk or ball can lids as visible markers to define the boundaries of this restricted area.
- Two players are across from each other at the net, inside the service line within the alley.

SEQUENCE

- Players volley back and forth within the restricted area, volleying for control and trying to keep one ball in play for a specified number of hits.
- After achieving the desired number of controlled volleys without a miss, players attempt to win the point by passing opponent, keeping the ball within the restricted boundaries. (PLAYERS MUST REMAIN ALERT AND REACT QUICKLY TO KEEP FROM GETTING "PEGGED"!)

FOR VARIETY

- As the players' level of skill progresses, the number of controlled volleys which must be hit before players are allowed to win the point can be increased.
- Players may compete to win a specified number of points, or compete for the best of three sets, 10 points per set.

Peg

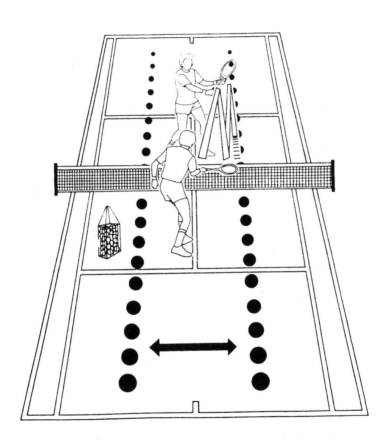

SKILL OBJECTIVES

- Full-court coverage in singles play.
- Making shots under pressure.
- Keeping the ball in play.

PROCEDURE

- Players are lined up behind the center of the baseline at one end of the court.
- Pro feeds from the opposite end at 3/4 court.
- Two targets are located on the service line near the singles sidelines.
- Two targets are located just inside the baseline near the singles sidelines.

SEQUENCE

- Pro feeds a 10-ball sequence to each hitter, moving the hitter from side to side and from the baseline to the net. Feeds should be varied so that the hitter must execute a variety of shots including groundstrokes, approach shots, half-volley, volleys, and at least one overhead.
- Aiming for a target on each shot, each hitter in turn hits a total of 10 shots as follows:
  four from the backcourt behind the service line,
  two from the midcourt area near the service line,
  two from the forecourt, close in to the net,
  one from the center of the service line, and
  one from close in to the net at the center line.
- Hitter then goes to pick up balls as the next player in line begins the sequence.
- After picking up 10 balls, player rotates to the end of the line.
- The same sequence is repeated as players continue to rotate after 10 shots each.

172

Perfect 10

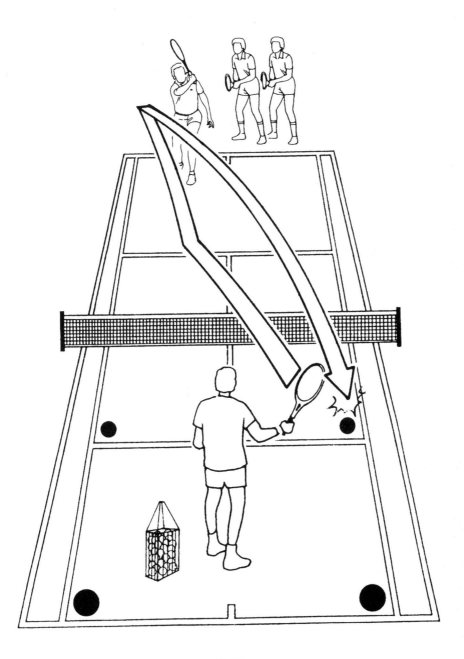

Doubles
Match-Play
Tactics

SKILL OBJECTIVES

- Closing in to the net in doubles play.
- Control and placement of volleys.

PROCEDURE

- Two players are on each end of the court in regular doubles formation.
- One end of the court is designated as the serving end, the other as the receiving end.
- Players on each team are positioned as if ready to begin a point with the server serving from the deuce court.

SEQUENCE

- Server and receiver close in to the service line and take split steps as server's partner starts the ball into play by hitting a forehand volley crosscourt to the receiver's partner.
- Receiver's partner hits a controlled volley down the line to the server.
- Server hits a controlled volley crosscourt to the racket, closes in from the service line, and takes split step.
- Receiver hits a controlled volley up the middle, closes in from the service line, and splits.
- Players continue to exchange controlled volleys until one player misses.
- Players then rotate clockwise and repeat the same sequence.

FOR VARIETY

- Receiver starts the ball into play bv hitting groundstroke down the line to server's partner and the drill continues as before.
- Server starts the ball into play by service receiver's forehand, then closes in. Receiver returns the ball down the line, then closes in and the drill continues as before.

Denmark
Doubles Drills

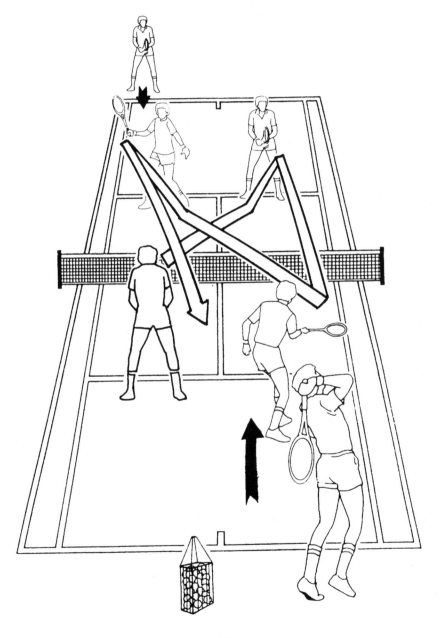

SKILL OBJECTIVES

- Crosscourt angles used in doubles play.
- Hitting under pressure.

PROCEDURE

- Net player is at the service line on the deuce side of the court.
- Baseliner is at the baseline of the opposite deuce court.
- Ball basket is located at the center of the net player's service line.

SEQUENCE

- Net player starts the point by feeding the ball crosscourt so that it lands behind the service line in the baseliner's deuce court.
- Baseliner hits a short-angle groundstroke crosscourt to the net player's service block.
- Net player closes in from the service line, takes a split step, and volleys the ball crosscourt.
- Players then play out the point hitting crosscourt only. NO LOBS ALLOWED.

FOR VARIETY

- Reverse: Repeat the same sequence from the ad side of the court.
- Baseliner may be allowed to lob after the initial return.

Keep it on the Angle

SKILL OBJECTIVES

- Touch shots and drop shots.
- Short angles at the net.

PROCEDURE

- Two players are on each service line, one player behind each of the four service blocks.
- Ball basket is located in the ad court alley near the service line on one end of the court.
- The player nearest the ball basket is the feeder.

SEQUENCE

- Feeder starts the ball into play with a drop- and-hit across the net into either service block.
- All four players rally the ball back and forth across the net within the service lines, using short angles, touch shots, spins and drop shots.
- Players continue the rally until someone misses.
- Feeder introduces a new feed and the rally begins again.
- After a period of time or a specified number of points, players switch sides to develop skill and consistency from both the deuce and ad side of the court.

FOR VARIETY

- Players attempt to keep one ball in play for as many hits as possible.
- Players attempt to win each point and compete as teams, one pair against the other.
- Players rotate after every 10 points.

Dink Doubles

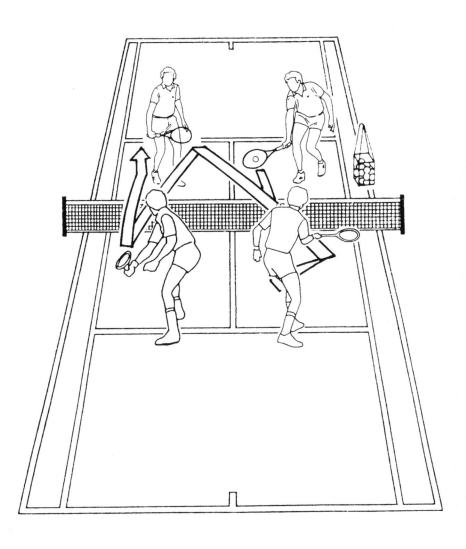

SKILL OBJECTIVES

- Covering the alley on a wide serve in doubles.
- Volleying to the open court.

PROCEDURE

- Two players are on each end of the court in regular doubles formation.
- One end of the court is designated as the serving end, the other as the receiving end.

SEQUENCE

(All serves and service returns are from the deuce court.)

- Server serves wide to the receiver's forehand.
- Server's partner at the net moves to the left to protect the alley.
- Receiver hits return of serve down the line.
- Net player hits backhand volley into the backcourt area behind the receiver's partner.
- Repeat for a total of four points.
- After four points, players rotate clockwise.

FOR VARIETY

- Reverse: Server serves from ad court wide to the receiver's backhand. Server's partner hits forehand volley into the open court.

Guard Your Line

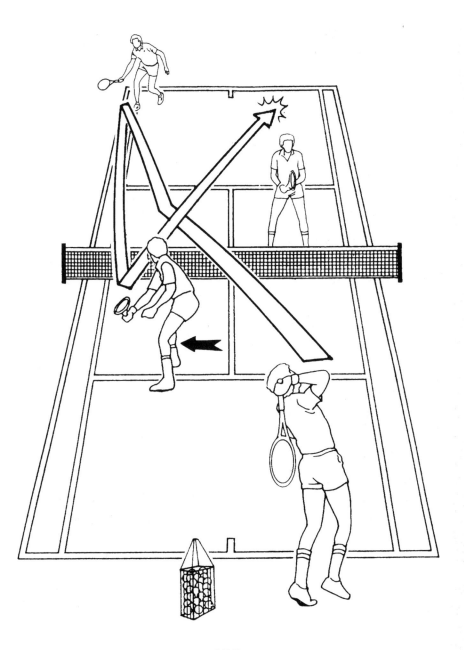

SKILL OBJECTIVES

- Poaching on the return of serve.
- Short-angle volleys off the poach.

PROCEDURE

- Two players are on each end of the court in regular doubles formation.
- One end of the court is designated as the serving end, the other as the receiving end.

SEQUENCE

(All serves and service returns are from the deuce court.)
- Server serves to the receiver's backhand.
- Receiver hits return of serve crosscourt.
- Server's partner at the net poaches to cut off the ball and hits short-angle forehand volley into the ad court alley to end the point.
- Repeat for a total of four points.
- After four points, players rotate clockwise.

FOR VARIETY

- Reverse: Server serves from ad court to ad court receiver's forehand. Poacher hits backhand volley to deuce court alley.
- Receiver's partner may attempt to save the point and players play out the point as if in a regular doubles match.

184

Putaway Poach

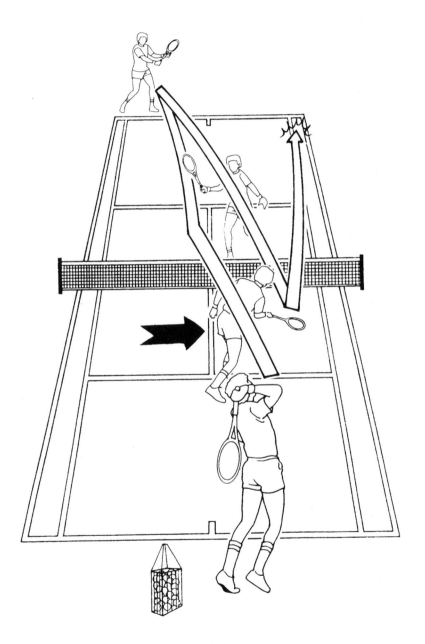

SKILL OBJECTIVES

- Doubles match-play skills.
- Maintaining concentration throughout the match.
- Regaining concentration quickly after play is interrupted.

PROCEDURE (6 players)

- Players are divided into two teams, one team on each end of the court.
- Two players from each team play at a time, in regular doubles formation.
- The third player on each team waits at the back fence until time to rotate in.

SEQUENCE

(One end of the court is designated as the serving end, the other as the receiving end. All points are served from the deuce court.)

- Server puts the ball into play by serving to the receiver and follows in behind the serve.
- Players play out the point as if in a regular doubles match.
- After each point, players on each team rotate counter-clockwise: Ad court player goes to the fence, deuce court player moves to the ad court, and "third" player becomes the server or receiver.
- Teams compete for a designated number of points, then switch ends.

FOR VARIETY

- Reverse: All points are served from the ad court and players rotate clockwise.

Bermuda Triangle

SKILL OBJECTIVES

- Closing in and split step.
- Approaching the net in doubles.

PROCEDURE

- Groundstrokers are positioned on baseline.
- Pro feeds from across the net, halfway between baseline and service line.
- Player A starts in the far corner of the pro's deuce court.
- Player A's partner is in the hot seat position.

SEQUENCE

- Pro feeds ball to deuce court.
- Player A closes in and splits.
- Groundstroker returns the ball crosscourt or down the line.
- Volleyer (Player A or A's partner) closes in, splits, and volleys into the opponent's ad court.
- Players play out the point.

FOR VARIETY

- Players rotate positions after each point.
- Players keep same positions for a specified number of points so that one team competes against the other to win.
- Pro alternates feeds to deuce and ad courts. Player A and partner adjust their starting positions accordingly.

Doubles Approach

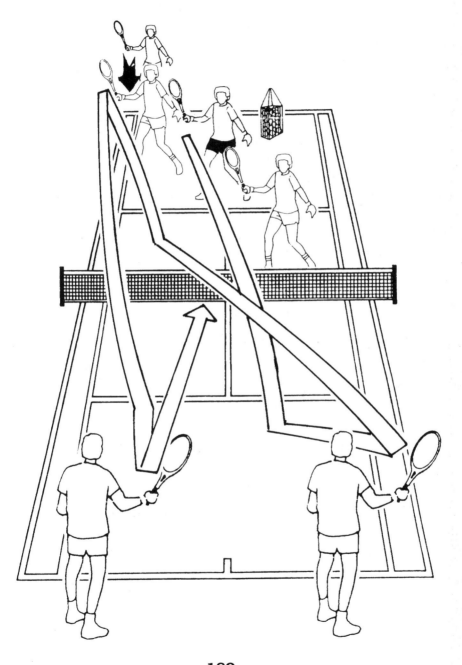

SKILL OBJECTIVES

- Poaching in doubles.
- Switching to cover the open court.

PROCEDURE

- Server is at the baseline in position to serve.
- Server's partner is at the net.
- Receiver is in position to receive serve.
- Receiver's partner is at the service line.

SEQUENCE

- Server makes good serve (no aces) and follows in behind the serve.
- Receiver hits controlled return of serve cross-court. Return should be tough for server to volley but not an outright winner.
- Server hits first volley crosscourt.
- Receiver's partner reads the direction of the ball and poaches to cut off the crosscourt volley.
- Receiver switches sides to cover the open court and the four players play out the point. The server's partner may poach on any ball after the server's first volley.

FOR VARIETY

- Players follow the same sequence for a designated number of points then rotate positions clockwise on the court.
- Players compete as in a regular doubles match but begin each point with the same controlled four-shot sequence as before.

Poaching in Doubles

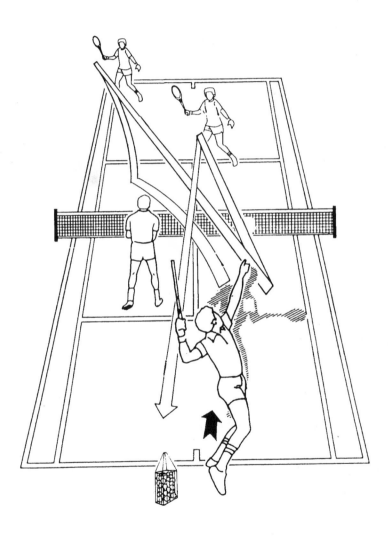

SKILL OBJECTIVES

- Maintaining good court coverage in doubles play.
- Moving in relation to the ball.
- Moving in relation to your partner.

PROCEDURE

- Pro feeds from deuce court service line.
- Pro's partner starts at the ad court service line.
- Receiver is on the service line across the net.
- Receiver's partner starts close in to net.
- Play is confined to the area of the court between the service lines and net.

SEQUENCE

- Pro feeds crosscourt to receiver.
- Pro's partner moves forward and receiver's partner retreats to service line.
- Receiver returns ball crosscourt to pro.
- Receiver's partner closes in to net and pro's partner moves back to service line.
- Pro returns the ball crosscourt again.
- Net player poaches and volleys ball up the middle for a winner.

FOR VARIETY

- Pro's partner attempts to save the point and players play out the doubles point.
- Pro moves to ad court and the drill is repeated with players adjusting their positions accordingly. The poaching net player will hit a backhand volley.
- Pro and receiver move to baseline and volleyers continue up and back movement.

Doubles
Net Movement

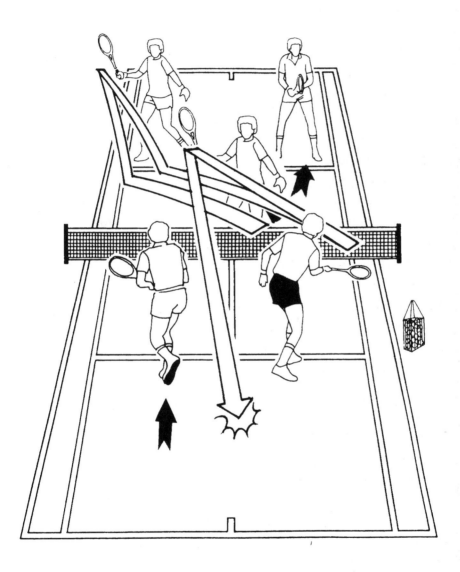

SKILL OBJECTIVES

- Serving for direction.
- Defending against the lobbed return.
- Court coverage in doubles.

PROCEDURE

- Server is in position to serve from the deuce court.
- Server's partner is in the ad court net position, as in regular doubles play.
- Pro is in position to receive serve from the opposite deuce court.

SEQUENCE

- Server serves to pro's backhand.
- Pro lobs the return of serve over the net player so that the ball lands behind the service line in the ad court.
- Server moves over to cover the lob and net player switches to hot seat position on the deuce side of the court.
- Server returns the ball down the line.
- Pro hits the ball up the middle.
- Net player puts the ball away with a volley.

FOR VARIETY

- Reverse: Server serves from ad court. Pro lobs over net player on deuce side of the court.
- Server moves over to cover the lob and hits short angle crosscourt instead of hitting down the line.

Serve and Lob Return

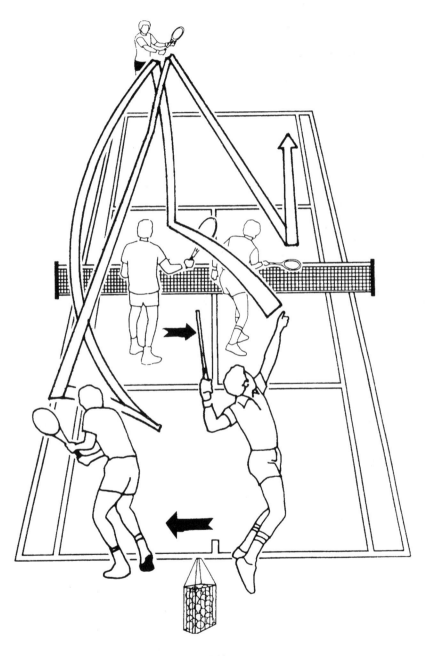

SKILL OBJECTIVES

- Racket control and quick concentration.
- Short angles and drop shots.

PROCEDURE   (6 players)

- Players are divided into two teams, one team on each end of the court.
- Two players from each team play at a time at the service line, one on the deuce side, the other on the ad side of the court.
- The third player on each team waits in the center of the court near the baseline until time to enter.
- Pro feeds from outside the ad court doubles alley, near the service line.

SEQUENCE

(All play is confined to the service area only.)

- Pro starts the ball into play for each point by feeding across the net to the deuce court player.
- Deuce court player returns the ball across the net to either opponent and players play out the point within the service lines.
- When one player misses, the player who has missed drops out and is replaced by the "third" player who has been waiting to enter.
- If one team wins three consecutive points, the players on that team rotate one position clockwise.
- Teams compete to win a designated number of points, then switch ends.

FOR VARIETY

- To emphasize control. Before winning the point, players must sustain a controlled rally until all four players have hit the ball at least once. Rotate after every two points.

The Mixer

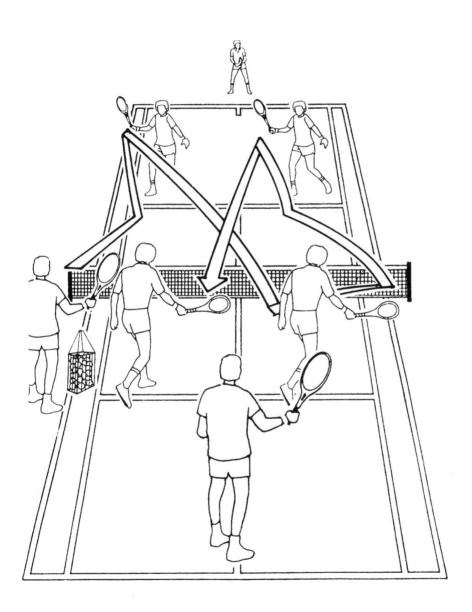

SKILL OBJECTIVES

- Covering the "hot seat" in doubles.
- Directing shots to the open court.
- Poaching at the net.
- Moving to cover the open court.

PROCEDURE

- Pro feeds from the baseline of the deuce court.
- Pro's partner is in hot seat position in the ad court service block.
- Receiver is on the opposite baseline crosscourt from the pro.
- Receiver's partner is at the net.

SEQUENCE

- Pro feeds crosscourt to receiver.
- Receiver returns the ball crosscourt to the pro.
- Pro hits crosscourt again.
- Receiver's partner poaches and volleys the ball up the middle.
- Pro's partner in hot seat intercepts volley and returns the ball crosscourt into the ad court left open by the poaching net player.
- Poacher's partner moves over to cover the open court and returns the ball down the line.

FOR VARIETY

- Pro feeds from the ad court and other players adjust their starting positions accordingly. Poacher will play backhand volley up the middle.

Hot Seat Drill

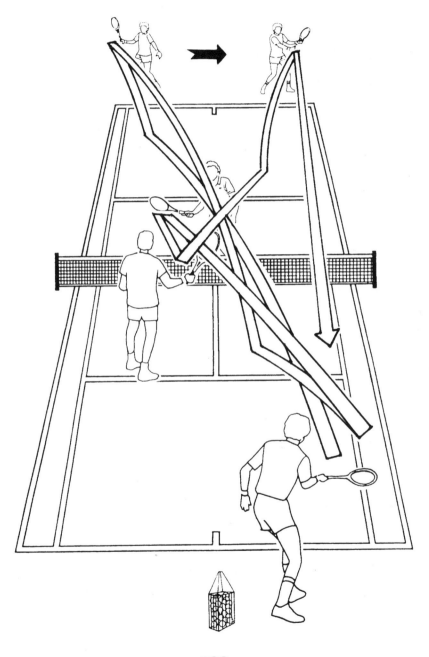

SKILL OBJECTIVES

- Control of volleys.
- Quick footwork and reaction time at the net.

PROCEDURE

- Four players per court, one behind each service square on the service line.
- Pro feeds from the center of the court, halfway between the baseline and service line.

SEQUENCE

- Pro starts the ball into play by feeding to either player across the net.
- Player volleys the ball back across the net to either opponent.
- The four players volley back and forth across the net, alternating volleys crosscourt and down the line, keeping one ball in play as long as possible.
- When one player misses, the pro introduces a new feed immediately so the rally can continue without interruption.
- After a designated period of time, players rotate one position clockwise and the drill is repeated.

FOR VARIETY

- To sharpen the angles and quicken the players' reaction time, repeat the same drill from inside the service lines, halfway to the net.
- To increase depth and control, move the players back to behind the service lines.
- With more than four players per court, extra players wait behind the volleyers and **a)** rotate in after a specified number of hits, **b)** rotate in any time a player misses a volley.

Four-Square Volleys

Speed
and
Agility

SKILL OBJECTIVES

- Serving for direction.
- Defending against the lobbed return.
- Court coverage in doubles.

PROCEDURE

- Server is in position to serve from the deuce court.
- Server's partner is in the ad court net position, as in regular doubles play.
- Pro is in position to receive serve from the opposite deuce court.

SEQUENCE

- Server serves to pro's backhand.
- Pro lobs the return of serve over the net player so that the ball lands behind the service line in the ad court.
- Server moves over to cover the lob and net player switches to hot seat position on the deuce side of the court.
- Server returns the ball down the line.
- Pro hits the ball up the middle.
- Net player puts the ball away with a volley.

FOR VARIETY

- Reverse: Server serves from ad court. Pro lobs over net player on deuce side of the court.
- Server moves over to cover the lob and hits short angle crosscourt instead of hitting down the line.

Running the Maze

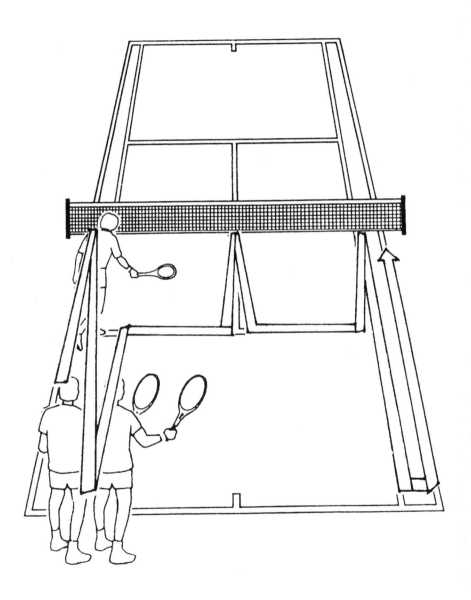

SKILL OBJECTIVES

- Physical fitness.
- Quick footwork.
- Changing directions forward and backward.

PROCEDURE

- Players start outside the alley at the doubles sideline.
- Players may line up along the sideline to race against each other or each player may race individually against the clock.

SEQUENCE

- Players start at the sideline and race forward to touch the next line on the court with their hand, back-pedaling to the starting line after reaching each successive line on the court. The race continues until all lines have been touched, coming and going, the full width of the court.

Running the Lines

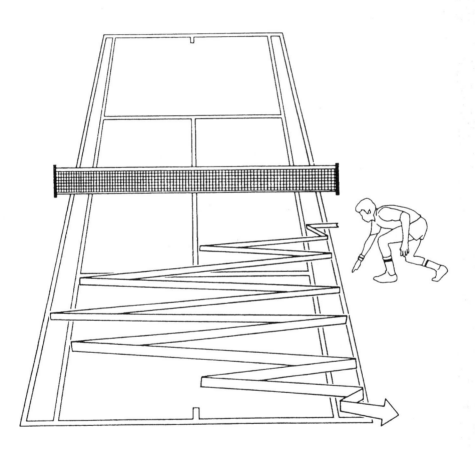

SKILL OBJECTIVES

- Wind conditioning.
- Strength in legs.
- Changing directions on the court.

PROCEDURE

- Player lays racket down 3' outside the doubles sideline and places five balls on face of racket.

SEQUENCE

- Player picks up one ball, sprints to the first sideline, and places the ball on the line.
- Player returns to racket and picks up another ball.
- Player sprints to next line along the width of the court and places the ball on the line.
- Player returns to racket and repeats the same sequence until all five balls are placed on lines across the width of the court.

FOR VARIETY

- Once balls have been placed on the lines, player must run to pick them up and return them to the racket one at a time, starting with the ball on the line farthest away from the racket.
- Players compete for individual times. Times are recorded and prizes are awarded for the most improvement in individual times.
- Sprints may be done over the width of two or more courts, instead of using just one.

Five-Ball Special

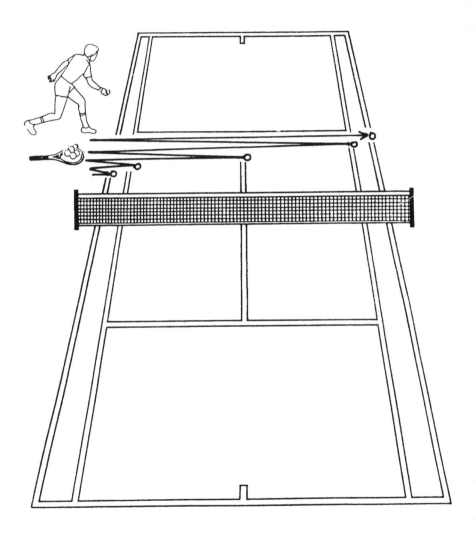

SKILL OBJECTIVES

- Quickness and agility
- Leg strength.
- Changing directions on the court.

PROCEDURE

- Four balls are placed on a racket at the center of the service line.
- One racket is placed in each of the four corners on that end of the court.
- Players line up in starting position at the sideline, halfway between the baseline and net.
- One player at a time races individually against the clock.

SEQUENCE

- When the clock starts, the player races to the racket at the center of the court, picks up one ball and runs to place it on the face of one of the corner rackets, then returns to the center racket.
- The player then picks up the next ball, races to another corner, places the ball on the corner racket and runs back to the center.
- Repeat until all four balls have been distributed, one to each corner racket.
- The sequence then continues in reverse with the player running to each of the four corners, collecting one ball at a time and replacing it on the center racket.
- When all four balls have been collected and replaced in the center, the player runs back to the starting line and the clock is stopped.

Four Corners

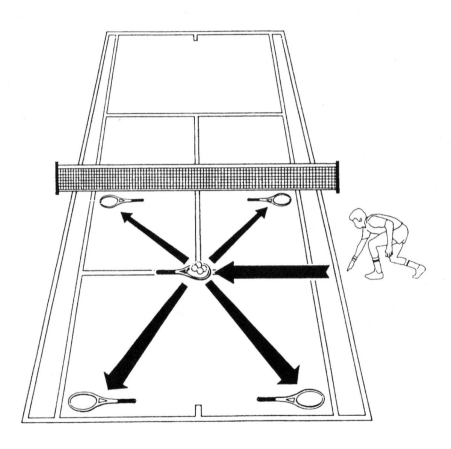

Ball Machine Drills

Each of these ball machine drills can be made more challenging or less challenging depending on the setting of the ball machine. To do this:

1. Increase or decrease the **depth** of the feeds.
2. Increase or decrease the **pace** of the feeds.
3. Alter the **direction** of the feeds to a slightly wider or less wide angle.
4. Increase or decrease the **interval** of time which elapses between one feed and the next.

SKILL OBJECTIVES

- Footwork and recovery on groundstrokes.
- Consistency and control of forehand groundstrokes.

PROCEDURE

- Ball machine is located on the center service line at one end of the court, halfway between the net and service line.
- Ball machine is set to feed into the deuce court.
- Players are divided into two groups, one group at each end of the court.
- Each group is lined up behind the baseline at the center of the court.

SEQUENCE

- Ball machine feeds crosscourt into hitter's deuce court.
- First player in line moves to the right, hits forehand groundstroke crosscourt into the opponent's deuce court, then recovers to the center of the baseline.
- Opponent moves to the right to cover the crosscourt return, hits forehand groundstroke down the line, then recovers to the center of the baseline.
- The same sequence is repeated once by the same two players.
- Players rotate to the end of the line after two shots each.

Cross to Line
Forehands

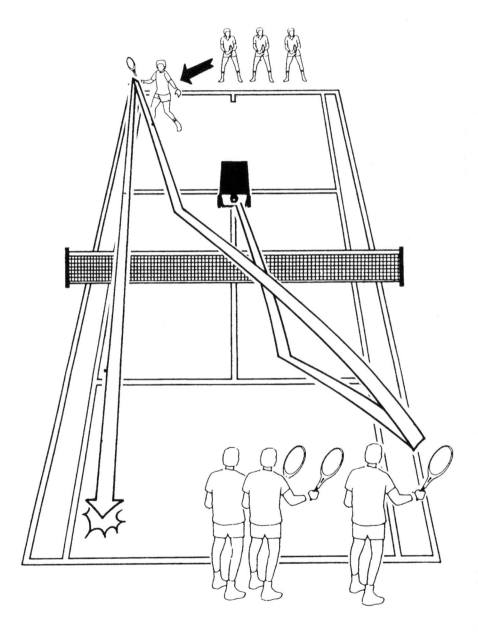

SKILL OBJECTIVES

- Footwork and recovery on groundstrokes.
- Consistency and control of backhand groundstrokes.

PROCEDURE

- Ball machine is located on the center service line at one end of the court, halfway between the net and service line.
- Ball machine is set to feed into the ad court.
- Players are divided into two groups, one group at each end of the court.
- Each group is lined up behind the baseline at the center of the court.

SEQUENCE

- Ball machine feeds crosscourt into hitter's ad court.
- First player in line moves to the left, hits backhand groundstroke crosscourt into the opponent's ad court, then recovers to the center of the baseline.
- Opponent moves to the left to cover the crosscourt return, hits backhand groundstroke down the line, and recovers to the center of the baseline.
- The same sequence is repeated and players rotate to the end of the line after two shots each.

Cross to Line
Backhands

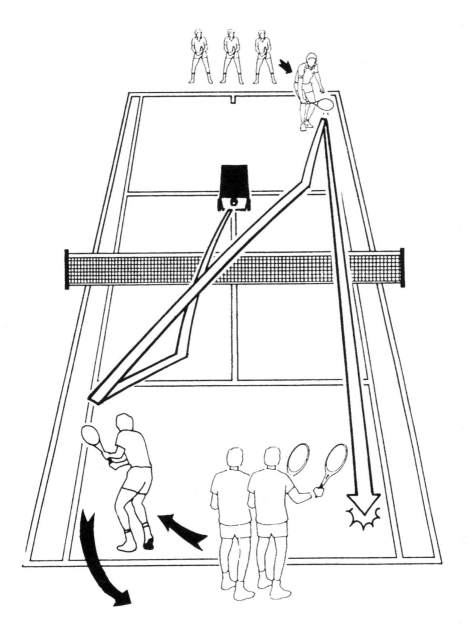

SKILL OBJECTIVES

- Footwork and recovery.
- Backhand groundstrokes crosscourt.
- Forehands down the line.

PROCEDURE

- Ball machine is located on the center service line at one end of the court, halfway between the net and service line.
- Ball machine is set to feed into the deuce court.
- Players are divided into two groups, one group at each end of the court.
- Each group is lined up behind the baseline at the center of the court.

SEQUENCE

- Ball machine feeds ball into deuce court.
- First player in line moves to the right, hits forehand groundstroke down the line, and recovers to the center of the baseline.
- Opponent moves to the left to cover the down-the-line return, hits backhand groundstroke crosscourt, then recovers to the center of the baseline.
- The same sequence is repeated and players rotate to the end of the line after two shots each.

Forehand Line
to Backhand Cross

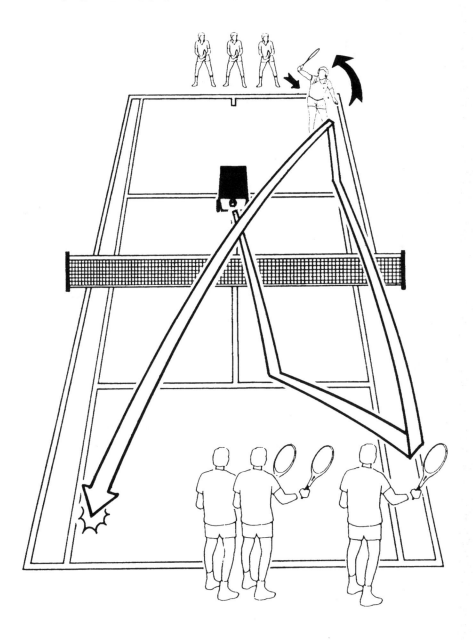

SKILL OBJECTIVES

- Footwork and recovery.
- Forehand groundstrokes crosscourt.
- Backhands down the line.

PROCEDURE

- Ball machine is located on the center service line at one end of the court, halfway between the net and service line.
- Ball machine is set to feed into the ad court.
- Players are divided into two groups, one group at each end of the court.
- Each group is lined up behind the baseline at the center of the court.

SEQUENCE

- Ball machine feeds into hitter's ad court.
- First player in line moves to the left, hits backhand groundstroke down the line, and recovers to the center of the baseline.
- Opponent moves to the right to cover the return down the line, hits forehand groundstroke crosscourt, then recovers to the center of the baseline.
- The same sequence is repeated and players rotate to the end of the line after two shots each.

Backhand Line
to Forehand Cross

SKILL OBJECTIVES

- Footwork and recovery.
- Forehand volleys.
- Backhand groundstrokes down the line.

PROCEDURE

- Ball machine is located halfway between the baseline and service line on the deuce side of one end of the court.
- Ball machine is set to feed crosscourt.
- Players are divided into two groups.
- One group is lined up behind the baseline of the deuce court, behind the ball machine.
- The other group is lined up along the sideline of the ad court service block, across the net from the ball machine.

SEQUENCE

- Ball machine feeds crosscourt.
- First player in line poaches to the right to cut off the ball and hits forehand volley into the opponent's ad court, then recovers back to the sideline.
- Opponent moves wide to the left to run down the volley, hits backhand groundstroke down the line, then recovers to the center of the baseline.
- The same sequence is repeated and players rotate to the end of the line after two shots each.

Forehand Poach
to Backhand Line

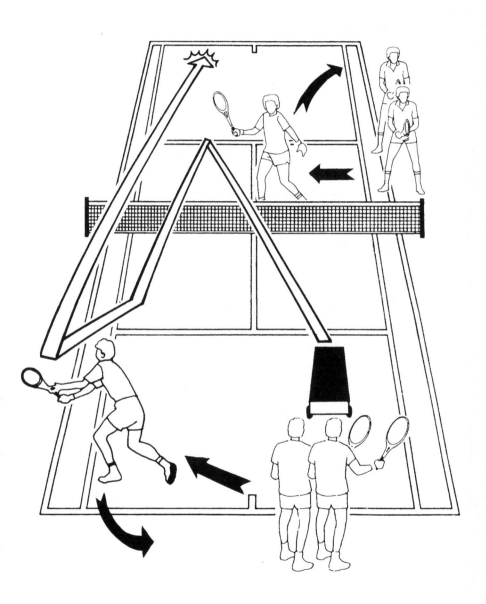

SKILL OBJECTIVES

- Footwork and recovery.
- Backhand poaching volleys.
- Forehand groundstrokes down the line.

PROCEDURE

- Ball machine is located at the service line on the ad side of one end of the court.
- Ball machine is set to feed into the opposite ad court.
- Players are divided into two groups.
- One group is lined up behind the ball machine, behind the baseline at the ad court sideline.
- The other group is lined up along the sideline of the deuce court service block, across the net from the ball machine.

SEQUENCE

- Ball machine feeds crosscourt into ad court.
- First player in line across the net poaches to the left to cut off the ball and hits backhand volley into the opponent's deuce court, then recovers back to the sideline.
- Opponent moves wide to the right to run down the volley and hits forehand groundstroke down the line, then recovers to the center of the baseline.
- The same sequence is repeated and players rotate to the end of the line after two shots each.

Backhand Poach
to Forehand Line

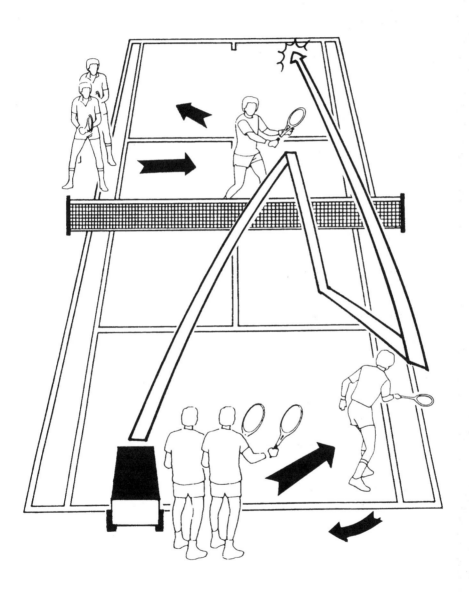

SKILL OBJECTIVES

- Footwork and recovery.
- Forehand poaching volleys.
- Forehand groundstrokes crosscourt.

PROCEDURE

- Ball machine is located at the service line on the ad side of one end of the court.
- Ball machine is set to feed crosscourt.
- Players are divided into two groups, one group on each end of the court.
- One group is lined up behind the ball machine, behind the baseline at the ad court sideline.
- The other group is lined up along the sideline of the ad court service block, diagonally across the net from the ball machine.

SEQUENCE

- Ball machine feeds crosscourt.
- First player in line across the net moves to the right to cut off the ball and hits forehand volley into the opponent's deuce court, then recovers to the sideline.
- Opponent moves wide to the right to run down the volley, hits forehand groundstroke crosscourt, then recovers to the center of the baseline.
- The same sequence is repeated, then players rotate to the end of the line after two shots each.

Forehand Poach
to Forehand Cross

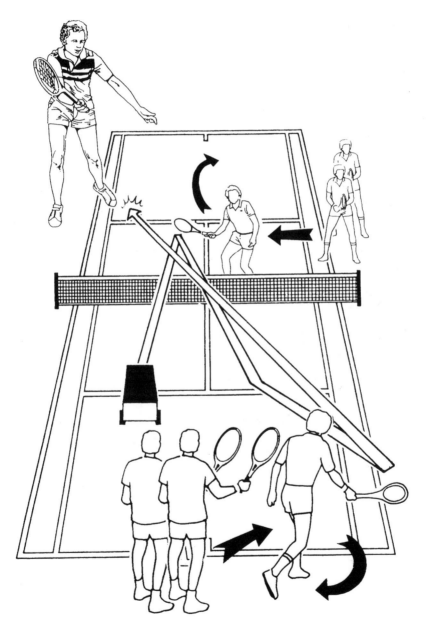

SKILL OBJECTIVES

- Footwork and recovery.
- Backhand poaching volleys.
- Backhand groundstrokes crosscourt.

PROCEDURE

- Ball machine is located halfway between the baseline and service line on the deuce side of one end of the court.
- Ball machine is set to feed crosscourt.
- Players are divided into two groups.
- One group is lined up behind the ball machine, behind the baseline near the deuce court sideline.
- The other group is lined up along the sideline of the deuce court service block, diagonally across the net from the ball machine.

SEQUENCE

- Ball machine feeds crosscourt.
- First player in line across the net poaches to the left to cut off the ball and hits backhand volley into opponent's ad court, then recovers to the sideline.
- Opponent moves wide to the left to run down the volley and hits backhand groundstroke crosscourt, then recovers to the center of the baseline.
- The same sequence is repeated, then players rotate to the end of the line after two shots each.

Backhand Poach
to Backhand Cross

SKILL OBJECTIVES

- Recovery footwork.
- Backhand approach and volley down the line.
- Forehand passing shots.

PROCEDURE

- Ball machine is located just behind the service line on the ad side of one end of the court.
- Ball machine is set to feed short balls into the ad court across the net.
- Players are divided into two groups, one group at each end of the court.
- Each group is lined up behind the baseline at the center of the court.

SEQUENCE

- Ball machine feeds short ball crosscourt.
- First player in line across the net moves in, plays backhand approach shot down the line, and continues closing in.
- Opponent moves to the right and hits forehand groundstroke back down the line in an attempt to pass the net player, then recovers.
- Net player closes in, takes split step, and hits backhand volley back down the line.
- Opponent covers the line and hits forehand passing shot crosscourt to end the sequence.
- Players rotate to the end of the line and the next two players in line repeat the same sequence.

Forehand Close
and Pass

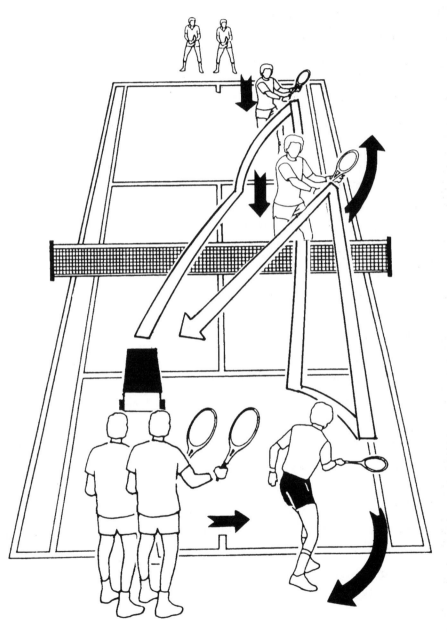

SKILL OBJECTIVES

- Footwork and movement.
- Backhand approach and volley.
- Forehands and backhands down the line.

PROCEDURE

- Ball machine is located just behind the service line at the center of one end of the court.
- Ball machine is set to feed short balls into the ad court across the net.
- Players are divided into two groups, one group at each end of the court.
- One group is lined up behind the ball machine, behind the baseline on the ad side of the court near the center mark.
- The other group is lined up across the net from the ball machine, behind the baseline on the deuce side of the center mark.

SEQUENCE

- Ball machine feeds short ball into ad court.
- First player in line across the net runs in, plays backhand approach shot down the line, and continues closing in.
- Opponent runs wide to the right, hits forehand ground stroke crosscourt, and recovers to the center of the baseline.
- First player closes in to cut off the crosscourt return, takes split step, and hits forehand volley into the opponent's ad court.
- Opponent runs down the volley and hits backhand groundstroke down the line to end the sequence.
- Players rotate to the end of the line and the next two players in line repeat the same sequence.

Backhand Close
and Pass

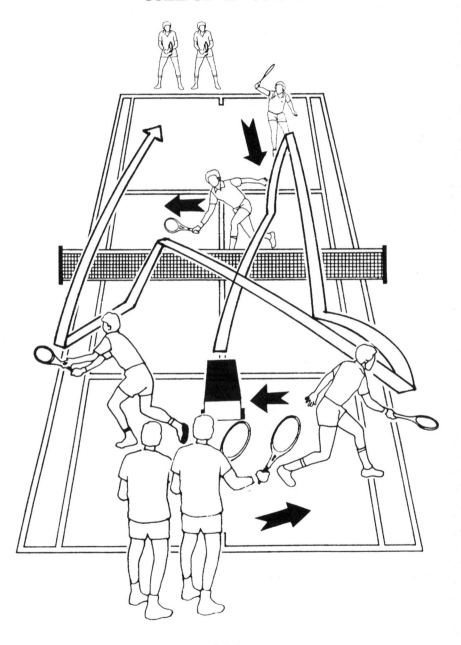

SKILL OBJECTIVES

- Recovery footwork.
- Forehand approach and volley down the line.
- Backhand passing shots.

PROCEDURE

- Ball machine is located just behind the service line on the deuce side of one end of the court.
- Ball machine is set to feed short balls into the deuce court across the net.
- Players are divided into two groups, one group at each end of the court.
- Players are lined up behind the baseline at the center of the court.

SEQUENCE

- Ball machine feeds short ball crosscourt.
- First player in line across the net moves in, plays forehand approach shot down the line, and continues closing in.
- Opponent moves to the left and hits backhand groundstroke down the line in an attempt to pass the net player, then recovers.
- Net player closes in, takes split step, and hits forehand volley back down the line.
- Opponent covers the line and hits backhand passing shot crosscourt to end the sequence.
- Players rotate to the end of the line and the next two players in line repeat the same sequence.

Try to Pass

SKILL OBJECTIVES

- Footwork and movement.
- Forehand approach and volley.
- Backhands and forehands down the line.

PROCEDURE

- Ball machine is located just behind the service line at the center of one end of the court.
- Ball machine is set to feed short balls into the deuce court across the net.
- Players are divided into two groups, one group at each end of the court.
- Each group is lined up behind the baseline at the center of the court.

SEQUENCE

- Ball machine feeds short ball into deuce court.
- First player in line across the net runs in, hits forehand approach shot down the line, and continues closing in.
- Opponent moves left to cover the down-the-line shot and hits backhand groundstroke crosscourt.
- First player closes in, takes split step, and hits backhand volley crosscourt deep into the opponent's deuce court.
- Opponent runs wide to the right to cover the crosscourt volley and hits forehand groundstroke down the line to end the sequence.
- Players rotate to the end of the line and the next two players in line repeat the same sequence.

Pass Again

- Controlling the direction of quick volley exchanges.
- Picking up eye contact with the ball quickly.

PROCEDURE

- Ball machine is located halfway between the baseline and service line on the deuce side of one end of the court.
- Ball machine is set to feed three balls in quick succession before an interval.
- Ball machine's partner stands at the service line in the ad court on the same end of the court as the ball machine.
- Opponents are at the service line in the deuce and ad court across the net.

SEQUENCE

- Ball machine feeds down the line to ad court opponent.
- Ad court opponent takes split step and volleys crosscourt to ball machine's partner.
- Ball machine's partner takes split step and volleys down the line to deuce court opponent.
- Deuce court opponent takes split step and hits winning volley crosscourt toward ball machine.
- The same sequence is repeated each time a ball is fed.

FOR VARIETY

- Players hit only forehand volleys.
- Players hit only backhand volleys.
- Players compete to see who can go the longest without making an error.

BALL MACHINE DRILLS

Quick Volley

SKILL OBJECTIVES

- Forehand approach and putaway volley
- Backhand approach and putaway volley.

PROCEDURE

- Ball machine is located inside the baseline at the center of one end of the court.
- Ball machine is set to feed a short ball to the deuce court, then a short ball to the ad court, alternating from one side to the other continuously throughout the drill.
- Players form two lines at the baseline corners across the net from the ball machine.

SEQUENCE

- Ball machine feeds short ball to deuce court.
- First player in line on the deuce side of the court moves in, hits forehand approach shot down the line, and continues closing in to the net.
- Ball machine feeds short ball to ad court.
- First player in ad court line moves in, hits backhand approach shot down the line, then closes in to the net.
- Ball machine feeds short ball to deuce court.
- Deuce court player puts the ball away with a forehand volley then rotates to the end of the opposite line.
- Ball machine feeds to ad court.
- Ad court player puts the ball away with a backhand volley and rotates to the deuce court line.
- Next two players in line repeat the same sequence and the drill continues without interruption.

FOR VARIETY

- Pro feeds lob to each player after the player has hit the volley fed by the ball machine. Player hits overhead smash.

240

Approach and Volley

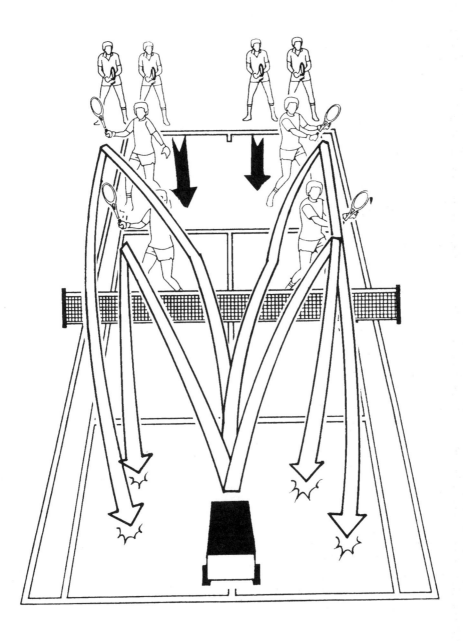

SKILL OBJECTIVES

- Closing in behind the serve.
- Reacting to the direction of the return.
- Putting away the second volley.

PROCEDURE

- Ball machine is located inside the baseline at the center of one end of the court.
- Ball machine is set to feed two balls before an interval, one to the deuce court and one to the ad court.
- Players are lined up behind the opposite baseline, near the center of the court.

SEQUENCE

- First player in line serves from the deuce side of the court and closes in behind the serve.
- Ball machine feeds first ball into deuce court.
- Player makes first volley and closes in to the net.
- Ball machine feeds second ball to ad court.
- Player takes split step, reacts to the direction of the ball, and hits putaway volley.
- Player rotates to the end of the line and the next player in line repeats the same sequence.

FOR VARIETY

- Players serve from the ad court.
- Reset ball machine to feed first to the ad court then to the deuce court. Players repeat the same two-volley sequence in reverse, serving
  (a) from the deuce court.
  (b) from the ad court.

Serve and
Two Volleys

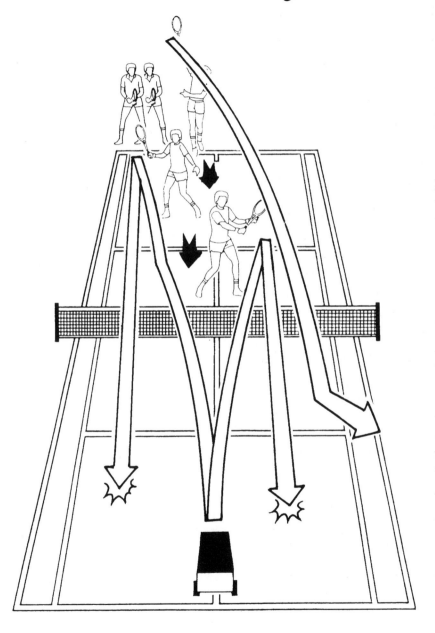

SKILL OBJECTIVES

- Closing in behind the serve.
- Reacting to the direction of the return.
- Setting up the putaway volley.

PROCEDURE

- Ball machine is located inside the baseline at the center of one end of the court.
- Ball machine is set to feed three balls before an interval — one to the ad court, one up the middle, and one to the deuce court.
- Players are lined up behind the opposite baseline near the center of the court.

SEQUENCE

- First player in line serves from the deuce side of the court and follows in behind the serve.
- Ball machine feeds first ball.
- Player makes first volley and continues closing in to the net.
- Ball machine feeds second ball.
- Player takes split step, hits second volley, and recovers.
- Ball machine feeds third ball.
- Player reacts to the direction of the ball, steps into position to volley, and puts the third ball away.
- Player rotates to the end of the line and the next player repeats the same sequence.

FOR VARIETY

- Players serve from the ad court and repeat the same three-volley sequence.
- Reset the ball machine to feed the same three-ball sequence in reverse, first to deuce court, then up the middle, then to ad court.

Serve and
Three Volleys

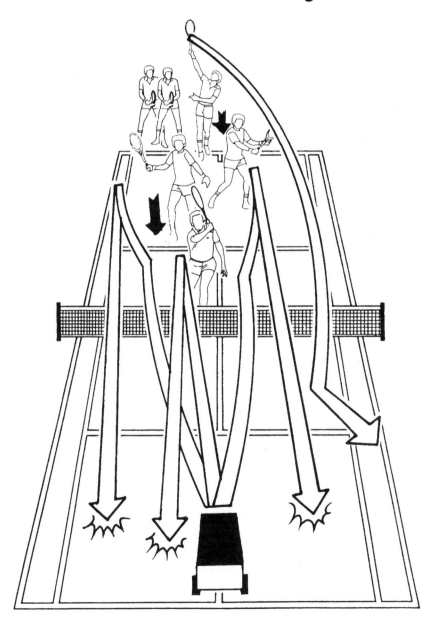

SKILL OBJECTIVES

- Placement of overheads hit on the bounce.
- Returning overheads hit on the bounce.

PROCEDURE

- Ball machine is located at the center of one end of the court, halfway between the service line and baseline.
- Ball machine is set to feed lobs with a high arc, to be played back after the bounce.
- Players are divided into two groups, one group at each end of the court.
- One group is lined up behind the center of the service line, across the net from the ball machine.
- The other group is lined up behind the ball machine, behind the center of the baseline.

SEQUENCE

- First player in line across the net from the ball machine runs forward and touches the net with his or her racket.
- Ball machine feeds lob.
- Player backs up, lets the ball bounce, and hits overhead smash into the deep corner of the ad court.
- First opponent in line runs down the ball and hits backhand groundstroke down the line.
- First player runs in and touches net again.
- Ball machine feeds second lob.
- Player backs up, lets the ball bounce, and hits overhead deep into the corner of the deuce court.
- Opponent runs down the ball and hits forehand groundstroke down the line.
- Players rotate to the end of the line and the next two players in line repeat the same sequence.

FOR VARIETY

- From the same formation, opponents return the ball crosscourt instead of down the line.

246

Smash and Save

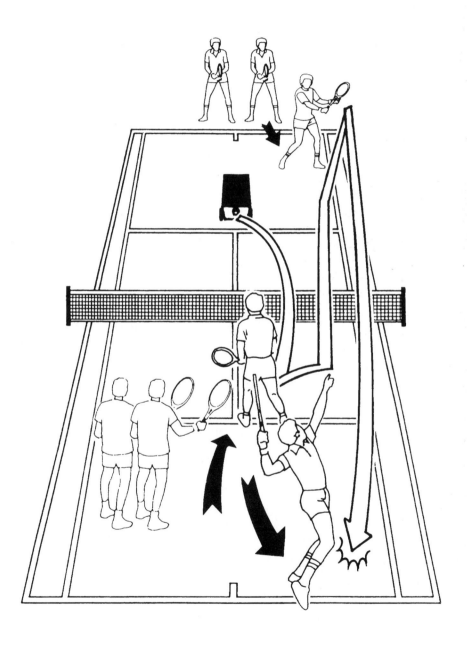

SKILL OBJECTIVES

- Footwork and positioning on the overhead.
- Placement of overheads hit out of the air.
- Returning overheads crosscourt.

PROCEDURE

- Ball machine is located at the center of one end of the court, halfway between the baseline and service line.
- Ball machine is set to feed lobs.
- Players are divided into two groups, one group at each end of the court.
- One group is lined up behind the center of the service line, across the net from the ball machine.
- The other group is lined up behind the ball machine, behind the center of the baseline.

SEQUENCE

- First player in line across the net from the ball machine runs forward and touches the net with his or her racket.
- Ball machine feeds lob.
- Player backs up and hits overhead out of the air, aiming for the far corner of the opponent's ad court.
- Opponent runs wide to the left and hits backhand crosscourt.
- First player runs in and touches the net again.
- Ball machine feeds second lob.
- Player backs up and hits overhead out of the air, aiming for the far corner of the deuce court.
- Opponent runs down the ball and hits forehand groundstroke crosscourt.
- Players rotate to the end of the line and the next two players in line repeat the same sequence.

248

Corner to Corner

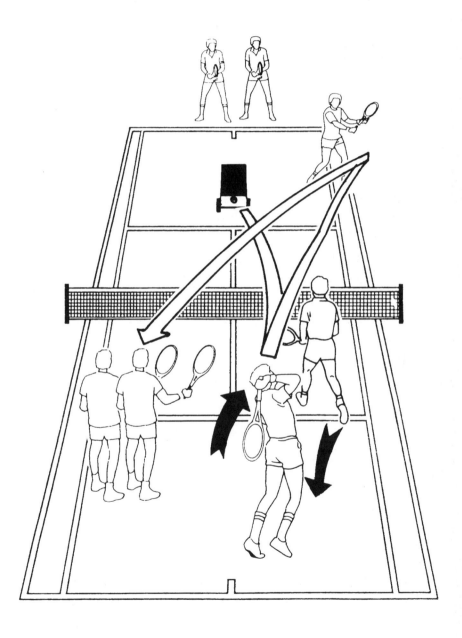

SKILL OBJECTIVES

- Footwork and positioning on the overhead.
- Placement of overheads hit out of the air.
- Returning the overhead down the line.

PROCEDURE

- Ball machine is located at the center of one end of the court, halfway between the baseline and service line.
- Ball machine is set to feed lobs.
- Players are divided into two groups, one group at each end of the court.
- One group is lined up behind the service line at the center of the court across the net from the ball machine.
- The other group is lined up behind the ball machine, behind the center of the baseline.

SEQUENCE

- First player in line across the net from the ball machine runs forward and touches the net with his or her racket.
- Ball machine feeds lob.
- Player runs back for the lob and hits overhead smash out of the air, deep into the corner of the ad court.
- Opponent runs down the ball and hits backhand groundstroke down the line.
- First player runs in and touches net again.
- Ball machine feeds second lob.
- Player backs up and hits overhead out of the air deep into the corner of the deuce court.
- Opponent runs down the ball and hits forehand groundstroke down the line.
- Players rotate to the end of the line and the next two players in line repeat the same two-shot sequence.

Bounce-Smash
and Save

SKILL OBJECTIVES

- Moving agressively from baseline to net.
- Hitting with power.
- Using momentum to generate power.

PROCEDURE

- Ball machine is located on the deuce side at the baseline of one end of the court.
- Ball machine is set to feed balls across the net into the deuce court to land halfway between the baseline and service line.
- Players are lined up behind the baseline of the deuce court, opposite the ball machine.

SEQUENCE

- Ball machine feeds ball into deuce court.
- First player in line hits forehand groundstroke crosscourt.
- Ball machine feeds second ball.
- Player closes in and hits half-volley or low volley from near the service line.
- Ball machine feeds third ball.
- Player continues closing in, takes split step, and puts the ball away with an aggressive volley down the line.
- Next player in line repeats the same sequence and the drill continues in the same pattern with players rotating to the end of the line after each three-shot sequence.

FOR VARIETY

- From the same formation, players hit only backhands.
- Players hit forehand-backhand-forehand.
- Players hit backhand-forehand-backhand.

Attack

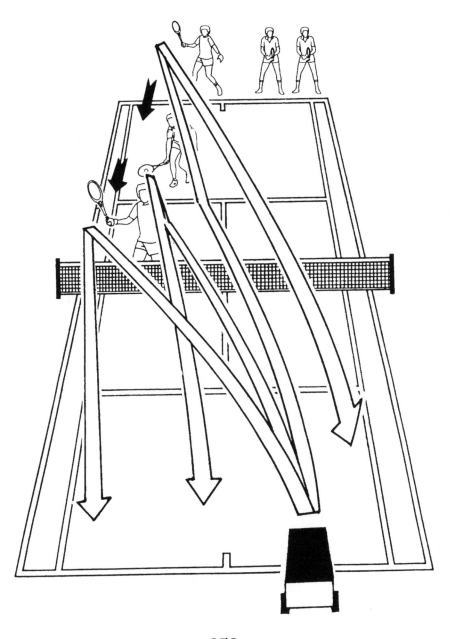

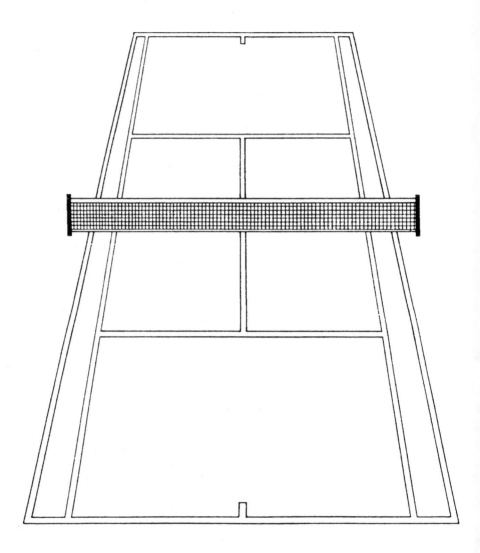

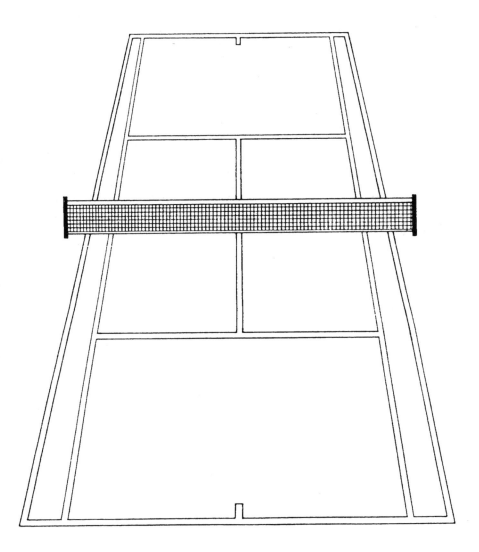

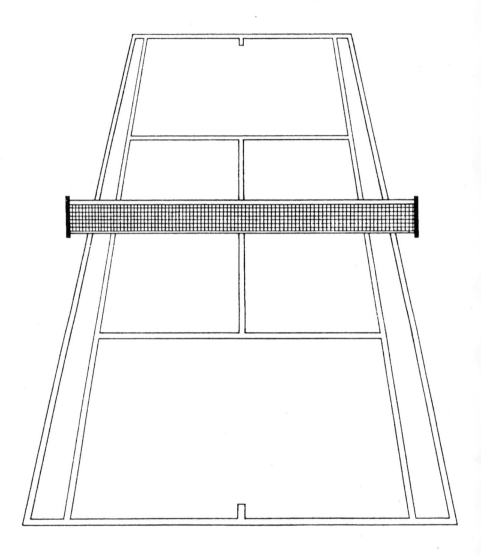